Magical Doors
The Symbols of Astrology

Magical Doors
The Symbols of Astrology

Jean-Marc Pierson

THE WESSEX ASTROLOGER

Published in 2023 by
The Wessex Astrologer Ltd
PO Box 9307
Swanage
BH19 9BF

For a full list of our titles go to
www.wessexastrologer.com

© Jean-Marc Pierson 2021
Jean-Marc Pierson asserts his moral right to
be recognised as the author of this work

ISBN 9781910531938

Cover design by Fiona Bowring at Bowring Creative
Typesetting by Kevin Moore

A catalogue record for this book is available at The British Library

No part of this book may be reproduced or used in any
form or by any means without the written permission of the publisher.

A reviewer may quote brief passages.

Thank you for being here.

Table of Contents

Preface		xi
Introduction		xv
1	A few things about Mercury	1
2	Understanding Venus	7
3	Hey! Mars!	9
4	Mother Moon	13
5	Here comes The Sun	19
6	The Big Jupiter	25
7	We don't have to like Saturn	29
8	Uranus: Expect the unexpected	33
9	Longing with Neptune	39
10	Under the surface and behind appearances: Pluto	43
11	Ouch! Chiron!	49
12	The Planet is the Actor; the Sign is the Costume; the House is the Stage	51
13	Metaphysics of the First House	55
14	Have your cake or eat it in the Second House	59
15	Magic in the Third House	63
16	Secrets of the Fourth House	67
17	The show must go on in the Fifth House	71
18	The witch's broom is in the Sixth House	77
19	Once upon a time in the Seventh House	83
20	Death in the Eighth House	87
21	Seeking for the truth of the Ninth House	91
22	Tenth House formalities	95

23	Flavour of the Eleventh House	99
24	Our connection with the Great Mystery: the Twelfth House	103
25	Analogy rather than equivalence	109
26	Aries	113
27	And then, Taurus	117
28	One, two, three... Gemini!	121
29	Cancer: All life starts in water...	125
30	Leo: Life is a spiritual show	129
31	Virgo: Almost ready	135
32	Libra: Balance is stronger than strength	141
33	Scorpio: Holding on and letting go	147
34	Sagittarius: Where is the grail?	151
35	Capricorn: Don't separate the fish from the goat	155
36	Aquarius: Fixed Air, really?	161
37	Pisces: The way up and the way down	165
38	Value of the fast moving things in the astrological chart	171
39	First things to look at	175
40	The worst way to interpret a chart	177
41	Don't push the astro colours back into the tubes	179
42	How to understand Black Moon Lilith	181
43	The lunation cycle as a clown story	183

Dedication

One day, instead of saying: "You should write a book!", a friend told me: "You have written one".

Thank you, Radilina Shanova.

Preface

This book was born from a blog.

The blog was born from people telling me "You should write a book!"

Those who were telling me this were reading my posts on Facebook. I was just trying to get some attention, as you do when you would like to get paying customers.

I had spent a few years studying astrology at the beginning of the new millenium.

I was born with an influential Uranus in the third house. Going back to school, being told what to learn, how to learn it, in what order and at what rhythm is just not my idea of happiness.

Next to Uranus in my natal third house, loosely conjunct to it, is Pluto. These two planets happen to run more than mere background programs in my astrological anatomy. I studied obsessively and absorbed intensely. I started with a textbook by Antares, a Belgian astrologer. I found out about karmic astrology through Laurence Larzul. I learned a lot thanks to the *Manuel d'Astrologie* by Andre Barbault and a few others.

My heroes were Liz Greene and Howard Sasportas.

I have become aware of the existence of controversies between ancients and moderns ever since. I keep evolving, however I remain faithful to a psychological and modern approach, which is especially relevant when the purpose of our practising astrology or consulting an astrologer is self-knowledge.

My Sun rules over my third house, and happens to conjunct Neptune. Studying like mad, I found myself so spaced out that I stopped altogether and decided to enjoy a more grounded lifestyle. Ten years later, I came back to studying obsessively, whilst keeping in touch with the earth working as a gardener.

Books are my favourite teachers. You meet them as if by chance. They become a voice that speaks to you, personally, as if the author was looking into your eyes. You can ask them to repeat, to shut up, to tell you more, you can wake them up in the middle of the night or invite them for breakfast. They have the utmost respect for your own particular rhythm.

Books are made of paper. Do you believe that materials carry vibes? Books are like healing crystals. They are talismans. They protect you from ADHD. Time spent with a book has a quality which is somehow the midpoint between looking at a screen and meditation.

I didn't think of writing one. I wanted to read more, understand astrology deeply, and translate charts for people, along with gardening, for a living. I created a page and a group on Facebook, and kept writing tweets, daily posts and interacting with people on and offline... People kept telling me "You should write a book!"

I started a blog instead. I started with Mercury. I needed to start with Mercury, Venus and Mars because they are more specific than the luminaries.

We usually read about the Sun and Moon first, so when I started to write about the planets, it felt more stimulating to avoid the usual procedure and start directly with learning a little bit more than what almost everyone knows already. For the same reason, I started with the planets rather than the signs...

However I didn't think much about the order. Maybe Mercury is the first energy we meet when we start writing or reading or talking with someone. Then Venus and Mars are also kind of intermediate between the outer and inner worlds. Then you may gain access to the Queen and the King. Then after the personal planets, on to Jupiter, Saturn and the wider circles...

Preface

Every now and then, we need to stop digging and take some distance instead. How do all these energies come together when we are trying to interpret charts?

A text is more than a juxtaposition of words and a chart is indeed more than a list of placements. There are famous examples of sentences that look almost identical with radically different meanings, like in the story of the panda who goes to a restaurant, eats, but instead of paying the bill, gets a revolver out of his pocket and shoots the waiter. Then it leaves the place. Panda: eats, shoots and leaves...

The two possible meanings of the word "shoots" stem from common ground. A young plant growing quickly isn't as quick as a bullet, but by comparison with the speed of growth of more mature plants, it makes sense to call them shoots. Unless it's the fact of initiating a movement in a new direction that makes us call shoots "shoots"?

If "ordinary" language can be so complex, we can expect the way astrological placements come together won't boil down to a boring list. However, I won't be able to come up with a whole set of grammar rules for astrological symbols in this book. The focus here is on the basic vocabulary. Planets, angles and signs are more than words. They are symbols.

Symbols mean something that comes from another dimension, which we can call "magical", with a poetic mindset, please. You can say "spiritual" if you prefer, or "astral". This dimension lives behind our everyday world of manifestations. It is hidden from plain sight, it is "occult". We could also say "abstract", provided we don't believe abstract realities to be somewhat less real than the world of particular manifestations.

The way to understand symbols, these magical doors, is contemplation. I hope I've been able to share some moments of wonder with my words.

Introduction

When I was studying psychology, I loved a series of lectures about the history of religions.

I learned that all spiritual traditions are symbolic languages. This is of course true of astrology. Dreams, fairy tales, fantasies, and poetry all speak in symbolic language.

Mircea Eliade was the historian of religion who popularised the word "shaman" and showed that indigenous traditions all over the world were essentially similar; he said that symbolic language is "consubstantial" with the human soul. Symbols are part of the stuff we are made of; they allow intimacy with the world of the human psyche.

Symbols don't obey the laws of logic we learned at school. Symbolic language has no articulated grammar, no clear definitions. Significations can be paradoxical, as life sometimes appears to be.

The fundamental rule is the law of analogy. Symbols don't tell, they show. For example:

Aries, whose symbol is the head of a charging ram, can convey anything with the characteristics of a charging ram. It may be the violence of a fist hitting a face, or the instinctive enthusiasm of a male individual for a female partner. It may mean attacking a problem, taking action, mustering strength, focusing and moving forward powerfully in any kind of circumstance. It can happen physically, emotionally, socially, intellectually or even spiritually. Like we say: "As above, so below" (and the other way round).

Never ask "What does this mean exactly?" when looking at a symbol. Symbols do not have exact meanings. They should be interpreted analogically.

Symbols give us clues. We are always deciphering riddles. A symbol might say: "What you are looking for is like me in some way..."

When reading charts, we need to know as much as possible about the context and use our intuition.

When we are not reading charts, symbols point out broad horizons and contemplating them is an essential daily practice...

These astrological musings have been written in this spirit.

1

A few things about Mercury

I like to think of the planetary energies as our *psychic organs*.

If we were studying anatomy, we would start learning about things that are true for every human being. For instance, whatever we may learn about the lungs and the human respiratory system would be valid for anybody. At this level of knowledge, we are all the same, and that's great; I could be hospitalised almost anywhere in the world and still be taken care of.

Now, we are also all different. Some people may have a huge respiratory capacity and others may suffer from asthma. Similarly, everyone has Mercury in their chart, but mine is in Libra, connected by aspects to Venus, Jupiter and Saturn and in the fourth house. However, understanding what is true for everyone is necessary before getting into specifics.

Planets can be summarized by key verbs.

Mercury says:

> *I think – I communicate*

If you remember only two key verbs, remember those!

If you're ready for more, Mercury also says:

> *I speak – I analyse – I imitate – I move – I serve – I pass on the message – I learn – I study – I reason – I read – I write – I trade – I exchange – I walk – I run – I speed up – I drive the car! – I do the DIY – I talk – I lie – I trick – I joke – I sing – I play music – I observe – I classify – I pay attention to details – I multiply – I divide – I count – I adapt – I adjust – I know – I repair – I link – I connect – I go get the info – I explore – I am curious about everything – I heal – I collect – I make lists…*

Mercury symbolises our mind! With Mercury, however, it is not a case of the mind, the entire mind and nothing but the mind though. More specifically, Mercury has a lot to do with our ability to reason, to use words and numbers and to apply common sense. And what is the mind, by the way? This is too big a question for now.

Mercury is also our ability to move.

Sometimes Mercury is the monkey mind. Sometimes it is the awakened mind with an ability to heal. When we talk about mind-body connection, we're talking about the magic of Mercury, the connector.

Planets can also represent people who appear in our lives. Mercury can represent a sibling, a young person, a peer or a neighbour.

It is associated with the age of 10 or 12, before puberty. At that age, children are interested in learning and knowing. They may know, for instance, every kind of dinosaur that ever existed, and look at you with pity if you don't know the difference between a Stegosaurus and a Pterodactyl. Later on, when boys become the main focus of girls and vice versa, the dinosaurs will lose their aura of prestige...

Do you get the spirit of Mercury?

At school, a child with a strong Mercury will be... Wait a little bit and try to guess before reading the next lines...

***

They will be good at school indeed, unless they are so clever that they get bored and distracted. The Mercury child could become the one that disrupts the class, cracks jokes or plays tricks, whilst being able to answer the teacher's questions correctly. Which, in their mind, entirely justifies the cheeky behaviour! They can also make a fortune selling sweets to their classmates.

When in love the Mercury teenager (or adult) will not be the most passionate or faithful, as curiosity for all that exists is their main motivation.

A few things about Mercury

For the Mercurial individual feelings are a very interesting subject to observe in others, and great to imitate in order to make everyone laugh, but being immersed in them... not too much, thank you!

The energy of Mercury makes you like things and people, but when you fall in love, it's not Mercury anymore, it's Venus or Mars. Now, when it comes to the business of the heart, Mercury can help a lot, as this energy knows how to communicate. Need a chat-up line?

What kind of jobs, what kind of hobbies would a Mercury person most enjoy? I will let you guess this one...

If Mercury was an animal, which one would it be? A squirrel maybe? Not a rhinoceros. A rhinoceros would rather make me think of a combination of Mars and Saturn. (Saturn gives the heavy, armoured twist to the Martian aggressiveness of the beast). Little birds, swallows, robins and carrier pigeons are indeed Mercury in animal form. Let's not forget the bees either.

When I was young, I read *The Adventures of Tintin*. Do you know him? He is quite Mercurial. He is a reporter, always on the move. You don't see him expressing an interest in women; he loves his best friend, Captain Haddock, and Milou (or Snowy), his dog. He is very clever. He is curious about everything. He always finds a way to get himself out of the most complicated situations. Mercury is your inner Tintin!

Let's now go for a walk along the street and look at the buildings. Which ones are we going to tag as Mercury?

The post office is a typical one of course. All the shops will be tagged as Mercury because Mercury is a trader. Yesterday I noticed two shops sitting right next to each other: one was a music shop and the other one a wine shop. I was thinking: it's a Neptune spot! Neptune, the planet of Pisces, is relevant to both music (music expresses feelings without words and connects us with other dimensions, or just offers a way to escape reality) and to wine (drink like a fish; it's liquid and also a way to escape reality!)

Now both shops deserve the Mercury tag – simply for being shops: places where exchange takes place. As you see, astrology, like life, has many layers.

Mercury, by the way, is also a musician: you need to be skilled and nimble-fingered to play an instrument. You need to be able to articulate well to sing. It's communication.

Another shop that expresses Mercury is the stationary shop. Here you will find all you need to write and do the accounts. The vet, the pet shop, that's Mercury again. The chemist, the dentist, the bus garage, the bus stops, the metro station, even the individual buses and trains, the pavements and roads... Everything that allows movement and communication is an expression of the energy of Mercury. Great journeys are usually associated with Jupiter, the sign Sagittarius and the ninth house, but short trips in the neighbourhood are ruled by Mercury.

The schools where young people attend lessons and mix with their peers are Mercurial places.

The physiotherapist and the health food shop express yet another side of this multifaceted energy.

In the body, Mercury rules the nervous system. It's all about communication, whether of orders from the brain to the muscles, or information from the senses to the central nervous system where everything is stored and interconnected.

It also rules the lungs (breathe in, breathe out, exchange with the environment) and the intestines (break down food into smaller constituents and sort out what to keep and what is rubbish). The collarbones, arms and hands are also under Mercury's rule.

We could look at life as a double movement. A movement from source towards the multiplicity of things and beings, and a movement from multiplicity back to source. Mercury expresses the movement towards multiplicity. It turns its back to the temple and looks at the world. In philosophy, he is all with Aristotle, and probably sarcastic about Plato.

Mercury values observation and experimentation over speculation and metaphysics.

We know all the energies intimately as we have been living them since we were born. All we need is to be able to recognize them and differentiate between them. Recognizing and differentiating are Mercury at work.

I leave you here to meditate...

Enjoy!

2

Understanding Venus

Venus attracts, charms, values, glues, enjoys, entices, loves, likes, feels, relates, sings, paints, decorates, dresses up, is beautiful, gets in touch, chats, socialises, eats... and owns.

Venus, like Mars, desires and makes love.

Venus wants to have. Venus wants to bind, to attach, to keep, to cast spells...

One of her favourite games is "Catch me if you can".

Venus brings social skills. The Goddess of love knows what makes things work between people.

When we tell others how beautiful, how great, how funny, how wonderful they are, when we say "You're a star!"; "You're a gem!"; or "You've done an amazing job!"; when we tell others that we are grateful for who they are or what they do, it becomes possible and even easy to get what as social animals we naturally desire: company, help, attention, protection, security and pleasure. We find friends, allies, companions and lovers. We know how to be with others. We hope they will know how to be with us. If they don't, we'll teach them! Venus knows how to bond...

To be able to value others we need to believe in our own worth. Feeling comfortable in our own skin helps a lot! If we feel insecure, nervous or self-conscious things won't work well. A compliment by an ugly duckling is not a compliment by a swan.

Ugly ducklings sometimes try to convince others that the ugliest ducklings are they themselves. It's understandable. It's terrible to be the ugliest duckling. If Venus is afflicted in our chart, we may get caught in spirals of negative valuation. We should do unto others as we would have them do unto us, because others usually do unto us as we do unto them.

If they do unto us as we did unto them and if the result is painful, we'd better come back and work on our own sense of self-worth, and maybe ask for help... Venus doesn't mind asking.

If there is only one key word to remember about Venus, it is *Value*.

We don't value intellectually. We like, we love, we desire, we admire... On social media, what we write is from Mercury, but the smileys, the likes, the loves, the laughs, the sad or angry emojis are from Venus.

If we remember only two key words, let them be *Value* and *Relationship*.

If you can remember three words, remember *Glue* as well. Mercury connects with no strings attached. Venus unites.

Ah yes, please, remember also *Harmony*. That's all Venus wishes for, in love, in bed and in art galleries.

Remember also *Enjoy*

Without pleasure, is life worth living?

Astrology is mental yoga. It consists of understanding energies to the degree that we can guess what happens when you mix them. The more we become familiar with what the planetary energies are by themselves, the easier it will be to understand how signs, houses and other planets sending aspects to them confirm or modify their expression. I hope you have enjoyed this Venusian ballad!

3

Hey! Mars!

When Mars speaks it says:

I do! I fight! I go get what I want! I desire! I compete! I attack! I start! I am first! I lead! I protect! Me want! I conquer! I stand for...!

Exclamation marks galore!!!

To get a better grasp on Mars, let's imagine characters.

How would a Martian child behave at school? Would he or she be calm and focused or unable to keep quiet for too long?

How would a Martian boy talk to a girl he finds attractive? Would he hesitate for ages or be direct and possibly inappropriate?

What kind of jobs, what kind of hobbies would a Mars person enjoy? Embroidery or boxing? Sitting behind a desk all day long? Joining the Firefighters? Washing the windows of skyscrapers while hanging at the end of a rope like a spider?

If Mars was an animal, which one would it be? Yes, a charging ram. What else?

A good way to learn about planetary energies is to observe life and put mental planetary tags on everything. For instance, walking along the street and looking at the buildings, which ones would we tag Mars? Probably not the church, which would more likely express Jupiter and Neptune. Mars tags go to the Fire Station, the Police Station, the Sports centre...

What parts of the body could we label Mars? The fists. The head as well. (Think of the expression 'rushing head-first' into something.) The muscles and the blood. (When someone or something lacks Mars energy, we find them a bit *bloodless*.)

Which emotions among these five are from Mars? Sadness, Anger, Joy, Worry, Fear.

When we see red, it's Mars.

In mythology, he is the god of war. This energy of aggression is not necessarily negative. When it's well mastered, we attack problems or tackle tasks rather than people, and we have sex only with consent. It's possible to live in peace with others with a strong Mars. Those who really need to fight can get into a boxing ring or practise martial arts.

If Mars is strong and we are unable to handle it, we suppress it. We push it back into the unconscious, and then either:

We are going to attract people into our lives who will express Mars for us, or

We may fall in love with a fighter, or attract aggressors and end up as victim.

Whatever energy is not integrated into our personality will be met through others... I'm sure that's how St George ended up fighting a dragon; he owned only half his energy. Without a dragon to fight, George would not have behaved like a saint, that's for sure.

Planets are energies. They are best expressed with verbs.

The *quality* of the signs – similar to energy fields – can be expressed with adverbs or adjectives. Any planet passing through Aries or Scorpio can be expressed using the following:

Strongly – aggressively – courageously – impulsively – passionately – intensely – rashly – sexually – assertively

... or using adjectives to qualify behaviours, we will say:

hot, dynamic, daring, straightforward, quick, strong, passionate, bossy, domineering, overbearing, rebellious, competitive, provocative, sexy, independent, egocentric...

Mars is the natural ruler of the first house. As there are controversies about the idea of natural rulership, if you don't like it then forget about it, it doesn't matter. What does matter is what they mean: Mars is an energy of self-assertion, and the first house shows how we interact with others and the world. If these meanings don't overlap, what does?

The cusp of the first house is the Ascendant in many house systems. The Ascendant, and the first house as a whole, describe our surface behaviour. As Mars is the energy that moves forward, tackles issues, confronts the world, likewise, the Ascendant expresses how we meet the world, new people and new situations and our first spontaneous reactions to anything that happens.

I leave you to your astrological meditation!

4

Mother Moon

The Moon is one of the 'Big Three' along with the Sun and the rising sign.

If our personality was a kingdom, the big three would be the three most important people. The Sun would be the King, the Moon the Queen, and the rising sign would be the Knight-who-interacts-with-the-outside-world-on-their-behalf.

Have you heard of the concept of sub-personalities? Usually we think of ourselves as one person, which we call 'me', but what if we were actually more like several people sharing one body? Have you had the experience of having a friend who you usually meet for certain activities, and one day they invite you to their home? There, your friend looks like they have become another person! You are discovering another facet of their personality...

The energies represented by the planets don't blend seamlessly; we can consider them as sub-personalities in their own right.

The Sun and the Moon are present in everyone's chart, so whatever our gender, we all have our fair share of masculine and feminine energies. Say yang and yin if you prefer.

Masculine or yang energies are expressed from inside out, they are creative, active, dynamic, self-centred. Feminine, yin, energies are receptive, reactive or passive, attractive, relationship centred. They become impregnated and give birth to new forms.

When we read a chart, we should always start by checking whether yang or yin is dominant. Traditional gender roles confused energies and people. Men used to believe they could express only the Sun and Mars; women were supposed to express only the Moon and Venus (as if all these energies weren't present in everyone's make up).

The Moon is our yin side. Our inside. The Moon is us when we are receptive, when we submit or surrender, when we let go, when we relax, when we relate to others and the environment. (In order to relate we need to shut up and be open to whoever or whatever is *not* us. That's yin.)

The Moon is how we are when we are at home, when we find ourselves in a safe environment, in private, able to express our emotions and be receptive to other people's emotions.

The Sun, by contrast, is how we are when we leave home and shine our own light in the world. The Moon is our most intimate personality, the vulnerable part of us. The Sun is not vulnerable. How could it be? He's all from inside out. No arrow can pierce the Sun's heart!

The Moon in a birth chart also talks about our own childhood, how we were as a child, how our mother was, or more specifically how our relationship was with our mother when it came to caring for and nurturing us, and even more specifically, how we felt about this relationship.

I don't believe that planets represent people. You will often read that the Moon is the mother. I understand the Moon as the nurturing function, which is, in most cases, carried out primarily by the mother. When our mother was forcing us to do things, when she was forbidding or punishing us, she was Saturn. When she was the great love of our life, she was Venus. When she was a role model, she was the Sun. When she taught us things, she was Jupiter or Mercury and when she was a rival for our father's attention, she was Mars! When our father was preparing food or telling a story before we slept, he was the Moon.

Now that we have grown up (if we have), the Moon represents our 'inner child' that is the most vulnerable and sensitive part of us. The Moon in our chart shows how we need to be cared for in ways that make us feel secure.

The Sun also represents our inner child but it's the creative and playful inner child which is symbolised by the Sun, not the vulnerable and sensitive one.

Here's the Moon in a few key verbs. If you remember only four, remember these:

I belong – I feel – I need – I nurture

If you can remember more:

I dream – I imagine – I remember – I am fertile – I am pregnant – I give birth – I change – I go round in cycles – I care – I long – I howl – I attract – I react – I feed – I eat – I share – I intuit – I absorb – I mother – I cuddle – I smother – I embrace

I like to repeat that everything in life is the expression of the fundamental energies of the zodiac. A great way to learn is to look around and put energy tags on things and people... Let's go for a walk in the street. What are we going to label *Moon*?

If you feel like being serious about learning, don't read the following straightaway. Go for an imaginary walk in a street and search for buildings, things and people to tag *'Moon'*.

Here are my answers:

Firstly, all the private houses get the *'Moon'* label. That's where families live!

The grocery shop, the supermarket... where the food is, put a *'Moon'* tag. A restaurant would rather have the *'Venus'* tag, because we don't *need* to eat there, it's a pleasure, or even a luxury. However, it's food, so a secondary *'Moon'* label can go there.

The shop called *'Everything for the home'*: *'Moon'* tag!

The nursery, the playground, anywhere the children are cared for, all get the *'Moon'* label.

A wedding shop! The Moon wants to belong, the Moon wants to get married. Big *'Moon'* tag for the wedding shop too! Let's also attach a *'Venus'* tag, as hopefully a wedding is a story of love and partnership between two people (*Venus*) and not just a story of having children for your parents to become grandparents whilst you are dealing with your in-laws!

A honeymoon gets a '*Venus*' tag.

In a hospital, the nurses get the '*Moon*' label. Their job is to care. The hospital itself is tagged '*Neptune*'. The doctors get '*Jupiter*' and '*Mercury*'. (Mercury is the specialist in health. Jupiter is the expert and the VIP.)

I told you Mercury was associated with the age of ten or twelve, before puberty. Actually, the Mercury stage starts as soon as we learn to coordinate our movements, learn to walk and talk etc. The Moon is associated with our early childhood, when we were just born and lived our most intimate and vulnerable moments. At that time, we were mostly soaking in impressions. Our personal unconscious is made up of the events and emotional memories we get from these early times.

The lunar temperament is sensitive, imaginative and impressionable. People with strong Moon energy can possibly be a little bit psychic…

At school, a child with a lot of lunar energy will be easily distracted and even disturbed if the atmosphere is not peaceful enough. They may well be a cry-baby. They will have a lot of imagination and enjoy stories. Their favourite subject will be history.

They will hear "You are too sensitive!" a lot during their lives, unless human beings eventually learn to respect sensitivity.

When not overwhelmed by family duties, a Moon person will enjoy staying home, cooking and eating good meals, not doing much, sitting on the sofa, stroking the cat, listening to music, reading or watching TV…

If the Moon was an animal… it could be a she-wolf, howling at the Moon. The Moon can be wild! We may find it hard to believe when contemplating an amorphous entity sprawled on the sofa eating tons of chips, but yes, there is an instinctive wild beast hiding in there.

The Moon could be represented by a hen as well. One day, on a farm, I saw a hen followed by ten little chickens. A young dog approached. The hen charged the dog and chased it away. I was really impressed by the courage of the hen.

Other than that, if the Moon was an animal, it would be a unicorn, a winged horse, a feathered dragon, a kind crocodile in need of affection, a teddy bear, or something like that... a fantasy. A chimera...

The element associated with the Moon, and with Cancer, the sign it rules, is water. It's all about emotions and feelings. Don't try to convince them with logic; kindness works better.

Do you get the spirit of the energy?

If you remember only a few things... remember:

> *Feeling – Mother – Child – Family – Belonging – Imagination – Memory – Emotions – Home – Instinct – Unconscious – Emotional and physical needs – Intimacy – Sensitivity*

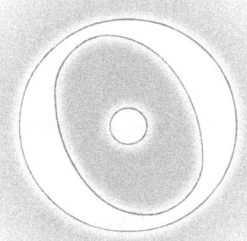

5
Here comes The Sun

The Sun symbolises the centre of our personality, our heart, who we really are. As the saying goes, 'We are not human beings having a spiritual experience, we are spiritual beings having a human experience'.

The Sun is the spiritual being within. The particular type of human experience we are having in this lifetime is represented by the sign in which the Sun was positioned at the moment of our birth.

A Sun sign does not represent a fixed set of personality traits. A Sun sign is rather a 'psychological landscape'.

For instance, stating "I am Capricorn" means something similar to saying "My life path takes me to the mountain". It is just a metaphor. On a real mountain, someone can be a climber and someone else a skier. One can be a mountain guide and another a hermit. Among climbers, some are going to be champions and others beginners. Mountain guides specialise: one will lead you towards wildlife, another will take you to the highest summits.

All we can be sure of is that whoever lives in the mountains will have to deal with slopes and a rigorous climate.

Have you heard of the concept of family resemblance, popularized by the philosopher Wittgenstein?

Imagine you're looking at a child and notice that he has the family nose! In this family, a number of individuals (but not all!) have a similar nose. Then you're looking at another child belonging to the same family, and you notice that he has the family eyes. Then you look at both children together. One has the typical nose, but not the eyes. The other has the typical eyes, but not the nose. They don't look like each other, but they both belong to the family, without a shadow of a doubt.

This concept of family resemblance applies to astrology. If your Sun is in a particular sign, you will express some typical traits of the sign and yet you may appear very different from other natives of the same sign. At a deeper level though, you will all have something in common.

I started this chapter on the Sun by talking about signs! Maybe the reason is that the Sun is the source of light. What is lit is not the Sun, but the world. When the Sun shines in the zodiac, what we see is not the Sun, but the sign, shining in a certain way.

The Sun symbolises the spiritual being we are. It is our heart, our self, the divine and creative spark within, whatever this may mean. It's a mystery!

However, the Sun has a big problem, which is that life on earth does not allow easy and spontaneous expression of our authentic self. We were born through the Moon – which is mother and matter (matter, material, mother are words built on the same root). Family, genetics, the influence of our early environments, our physical and emotional needs and conditioning, our past and lineage are all symbolized by the Moon.

However, the Sun, the inner divine spark, the spiritual being at the core of the earthly personality, embarks on a heroic journey. The challenge is: *'Become who you really are!'*

This quest for authenticity makes us walk on the path represented by the Sun sign. It is the sign of our aspirations.

The environment protects, nurtures and conditions us. The Sun is our inner guidance, what we want to become (whatever our past might have been), our spiritual instructions so to speak. Through the Moon we are influenced by the past, through the Sun we are called.

The Sun also symbolises the ego. The ego is the temporary compromise between the higher self (who we really are in spirit) and the conditioning imposed by family, society and material conditions... It's ourselves in a state of incomplete integration.

On its way to becoming *enlightened* the Sun-ego looks up at role models and seeks for ideals to identify with. The Sun in the chart says something about our ideals and role models, and about the spiritual qualities we need to become like them in our own unique way: consciousness and will power. Are you familiar with the principle put forward by the psychologist Emile Coué?

> *When imagination and will power conflict, imagination always wins.'*

In astrological terms, this translates as: '*When the Moon (imagination) and the Sun conflict, the Moon always wins*'.

Our conscious willpower struggles to break free... and the Moon always wins, until our little ego-based consciousness understands that it can't grow unless it plays by the rules and surrenders. In other words, we can't neglect our bodies and emotional needs and thrive as spiritual beings here on earth.

The potter can't make beautiful pots without surrendering to the nature of clay. We are not here to leave the material world behind, but to shape it according to our vision. This can't be done without respect for the feminine side of life.

The Sun symbolises the father, as the father, for a small child, is the first one who represents 'beyond mother'. Anyone who sets an example, introduces the world beyond the cocoon of safety and serves as a role model is symbolized by the Sun.

I hope I have explained the Sun with adequate clarity, however astrology does not give easy answers to all the great metaphysical questions.

For now, try to remember at least a few key words:

> *Heart – Spiritual core – Self – Willpower – Consciousness – Ideals – Father – Role models – Ego*

After the question *'What is it?'* I'll now set out to give some answers to the other great question: *'How is it?'*

Some personalities are more solar than others. Leo is the solar sign, but people born under other Sun signs can also be very solar if the Sun is well aspected (for instance if the Sun is conjunct an angle in the birth chart).

Like every other planet-energy the Sun can be summarised by a few key verbs. The Sun says:

I want – I create – I express myself

If you remember only three key verbs, remember those!

If you're ready for more, the Sun also says:

I show – I play (we can play like children having fun, or play like a musician playing an instrument or an actor interpreting a role in a play). When we have fun and play, we are spontaneously acting out who we really are.

I want (as opposed to 'I need')

I love (true love can only come from the authentic self)

I educate – I show the example – I lecture

I shine – I attract attention – I lead – I reign – I govern – I illuminate – I have fun – I entertain

When the Sun appears as a person we will encounter:

Someone with great vitality and charisma. Anyone with a royal attitude. A king of sorts.

– A teacher, a comedian, a musician (the band leader or the soloist) an artist, anyone performing, exhibiting, creating, showing… (possibly showing off).

– A father, an educator, a role model – a boss, someone in power, an authority figure.

– A saint, with a solar golden halo above their head!

As a lover, a solar individual will attach great importance to courtship. Love is a game and the greatest opportunity to value the ego!

If your idea of the perfect lover is someone who offers the greatest quality of empathy, the solar person may not be the best choice, unless they have enough water in their chart. The Sun will warm you up, but maybe ask the Moon for a deep understanding of what's going on in the secret corners of your soul.

The Sun gives warmth and light from the inside out – its nature is not to be on the receiving end. The Sun is fire, yang, masculine energy; there will be nothing petty in the solar individual's attitude. You can expect loyalty, support and generosity.

Please remember that no human being is a pure type. Everyone has the Moon somewhere! An absolutely pure solar type would give everything and receive nothing but praise, like a creator God.

If the Sun was an animal, of course, it would be a lion. He's powerful, he's beautiful, and everyone pays attention: the zebras, the antelopes, the hyenas, the other lions. Whether he sleeps, farts or wanders around, everyone knows what's going on. Paying attention to the powerful is wisdom!

Let's now go for a walk in the street and look at the buildings. Which ones are we going to tag *'Sun'*?

Let's not waste time in the suburbs, let's head straight for the centre. Here is the big square with all the fountains, the columns and statues!

A theatre, a gallery, a luxury hotel with people in costumes standing at the door...

The goldsmiths, the jewellers get their *'Sun'* tag.

A circus, a carnival, a concert hall are all Sun (or Leo) spots.

The movies will get a double tag; *'Sun'* because there are stars and it's an art, and *'Neptune'* because we go there to escape reality and get carried away.

If the Sun was a musical instrument, he would be a trumpet. If he was a kind of music, he would be something grandiose, like *Aida*. Now, if the Sun was meeting Uranus, instead of Verdi you would get free jazz or contemporary music.

By contrast, if the Moon was music, she would be romantic, sensitive, delicate, sounding like a tearful cuddle by moonlight, a serenade perhaps. And if the Moon met Uranus and turned to jazz, she would evoke the nocturnal life of human emotions with blue notes.

6

The Big Jupiter

Are you familiar with 'Miracle Grow'? It's plant food. How those plants grow! It's incredible! This may be the worst of all my metaphors, as Miracle Grow is not organic. However, for an introduction to Jupiter, it's pretty perfect.

A more traditional picture would have been the cornucopia, symbol of abundance. It was one of Amalthea's horns, the goat who fed Zeus when the future king of the gods was a child... Whatever you'll get out of it, expect to get plenty! Everything Jupiter touches becomes big. If you have a big ego, add a bit of Jupiter and you'll get a Mega Big Ego. If Jupiter touches your Venus and you're a painter, you're likely to paint something big, like the Sistine Chapel. In Michelangelo's chart, there is a tight square between Venus and Jupiter.

If Jupiter touches your Mars, you're not going to be just a mere warrior. You're going to be a Genghis Khan. Ah, maybe I'm exaggerating a little bit. Not everyone with Mars-Jupiter contacts becomes a fierce conqueror of the world, fortunately.

If Jupiter touches your Moon, your imagination will take you there and back. Your memory will be that of an elephant, and your emotions an ocean. Maybe you'll get a big stomach as well, as the Moon rules it.

If Jupiter touches your Mercury, you'll be clever: you'll see the big picture and talk abundantly about it. In fact you won't just talk; you will make speeches.

Mercury moves around, Jupiter travels the world. Mercury analyses, Jupiter synthesises. Mercury gathers information, Jupiter organises it into theories. Beyond what can be known by direct observation, logic and reason, Jupiter uses intuition and trusts he's right. Jupiter believes. Mercury is common sense, Jupiter is philosophy.

Jupiter and Mercury both symbolise the mind, but Jupiter's potent energy comes from a place of positive attitude, of coherence, of faith, of open mindedness. To be honest, I don't know whether our inner attitude is entirely responsible for our good or bad luck. What I know for sure is that it's an important factor.

If I used verbs to conjure up what Jupiter does, apart from *'I grow big'* I would say:

I rule – I integrate – I make laws – I know – I guide – I teach – I preach – I speak in public – I explore – I discover – I seek for coherence – I seek for meaning – I think

The three most important key words might be:

Integrate – Explore – Know

When Jupiter dresses up, he wears the robe and the wig of a magistrate, the square hat and gown of the scholar, the mitre of the Pope, the cassock of the clergyman, the lab coat of a scientist, a business suit, the uniform of the general or the outfit which usually goes with an appellation: *Your Honour, Your Holiness, Sir, General, Doctor…*

With Jupiter we have a function. We integrate society. We play our role. In a horoscope, Jupiter tells something about how we do that. According to Michel Gauquelin, who did a lot of statistical research to prove astrology was nonsense and found out that it was not, Jupiter is prominent in the charts of many politicians and actors. Playing a role is what these two categories have in common: they *represent*.

Jupiter is often said to bring good luck. However, luck rarely presents itself in the form of food falling directly from the sky right onto our plate. (I have seen a case, but it's exceptional).

If someone integrates into society by joining the local football team or charity or by going to church, and proves themselves a good fellow, the soul mate or the dream job may be found in this context. With Jupiter we integrate into society and in the process add our contribution to it. In return we receive opportunities and protection.

Let's now have a look at the shadow side of this energy... When a planet is *afflicted* in a chart it receives many tense aspects, or rules – or is ruled – by other afflicted planets; in this case it's likely that the shadow side is calling for some conscious tweaking.

The story of tulip mania in the 17th century is a fabulous illustration of Jupiter going wrong. All opponents to unregulated capitalism will agree with the necessity of Saturnian regulation to control boundless Jupiterian growth and hunger for profit. I love this story, maybe because I'm a gardener. It's the common story of all speculative bubbles. Back in the 16th century tulip bulbs arrived in the Dutch Republic and soon became very fashionable – so fashionable that everyone wanted some. There was more demand than supply so the price of the bulbs went up. Because the price went up, people bought bulbs, not to plant them but to sell them later and make a profit. With more people wanting to buy, the prices kept going up. Speculation went wild, so much so that the price of a single bulb reached ten times the annual income of a skilled worker.

At some point, buyers wanted to sell to make their profit. The more they wanted to sell the more the prices dropped. Eventually no one wanted to buy bulbs anymore, and the last buyers left with supplies were ruined.

I find this fascinating. Coming back to psychology and astrology, with an afflicted Jupiter, we may invest emotionally in our own ego and allow it to become inflated enough that we lose touch with reality...

Donald Trump has a retrograde Jupiter conjunct Chiron square Saturn, Mercury and Venus, also trine Sun and sextile Moon.

He inflated his ego as much as he could, but here is not the place for a debate about political ideas. I am talking only about the style of the public character. He is too much.

So, remember, Jupiter is:

Growth – Social Integration – Attitude – Role Playing – Mind – Quest for Meaning – Wisdom – Knowledge – Philosophy – Enthusiasm – Confidence – Faith – Travel – Exploration

7

We don't have to like Saturn

Jupiter and Saturn can be seen as two faces of the same coin. Called 'social planets' they symbolise the attitudes, beliefs or values we hold as members of a society with its rules and laws. A 'code of honour', a certain attitude towards traditions and customs, thoughts about duties and rights are examples of social values. Venusian values are tastes, likes and dislikes. Social values harmonise more or less easily with individual preferences. Jupiter and Saturn also speak about our religious, ethical or spiritual attitudes in regard to our place in the grand scheme of things.

If Jupiter expands whatever it touches, Saturn does the opposite. Saturn contracts, tightens, structures, tests, shrinks, condenses, slows down...

When it comes to feelings, Jupiter brings about enthusiasm and optimism, and Saturn fear and... let's say realism!

Saturn was called the 'Great Malefic' by traditional astrologers. Saturn brings difficulties. Would you wish a child to live a life without any difficulties to overcome? We are children of Heaven and Earth. They give us Saturn. We don't like it. We don't have to.

When Saturn touches Mercury, our mind may become heavy, stupid and slow; we may find it difficult to communicate, because of a stammer, or dyslexia, or autism, or shyness. Our mobility may be reduced, or we may become very logical, realist, coherent, consistent or serious. At school, children with Saturn square Mercury are either the best or the worst of the class.

When Saturn touches the Moon, we may suffer from emotional inhibitions and frustrations. Our mother may have been quite stern, our parents may have been very focused on good manners and behaviour and not very tactile, or just frustratingly absent. We may be very self-contained, or emotionally crushed.

There are of course many more possible interpretations than the few examples I'm giving here. Symbols are magical doors. They don't always open onto the same scenery, and there is always room for surprise. Life is more varied than the understanding of the wisest humans. All the places a particular magical door can lead you to have something in common, but this common something is from the spiritual dimension, just beyond the grasp of the rational mind.

One day Saturn will tell you about skin, bones and joints and another day about boundaries, structures and morality. The next time you open the Saturn door, all you may get is a great feeling of fear and inadequacy. If you're courageous enough to open it again, you may find yourself at the top of the social ladder or honoured for your achievements, but then, the day after, you're a hermit contemplating heavenly sights; and then the following day, you are home, because that's where your responsibilities are. You are telling the children how to behave: you say "YOU MUST" or "YOU HAVE TO" and often you say "NO! NO! NO!" but you are fair, and they know they can rely on you... Can you figure out the common thread?

All we can do with symbols and energies is to try to understand *in spirit*. However, if understanding in spirit is reading between the lines, then without Saturn, there would be no lines! Saturn wants a proper formulation.

Saturn is the energy that brings us down from spirit to the material plane; concretisation, materialisation, crystallisation... It's about taking form and keeping it.

Saturn's Greek name is Chronos, which means time. Time is our limit. We can't do and be everything. We need to make choices, and stick to them. This can feel very frustrating. Men may desire to love all the women they feel attracted to, like Jupiter does in his mythical world. That could be a fantastic plan, but in reality, there is not enough time and only a few ladies would consent. Each choice, each commitment implies a renouncement. With Saturn, we need to face reality...

When the potter makes pots, the clay is wet and malleable. Then the pot is left to dry and cooked and the form will be fixed until it's broken; if the pot we've made is square, it's too late to make it round; if it's round, it's too late to make it square. This is how Saturn works. Real pots, unlike dreams and ideas, can't be one day round and square the next.

Saturn rules the stern side of education, which is concerned with moulding behaviour. "Sit straight, do your homework, say hello, please, thank you and sorry (even if you are not really sorry), don't lie (unless it's politeness), don't steal, don't touch your genitals in public, get up early, be on time, respect others," etc. When Saturn becomes excessive, there is no capacity left for being emotional or spontaneous, and we end up living in an emotional straitjacket. But without Saturn, nothing in us would be firm enough to keep us standing on our feet.

Saturn brings things which can be painful but necessary. One day the baby has sucked enough milk from mother's breast. Baby's teeth are growing. It's weaning time. These wonderful moments will never happen again. Saturn closes the door and turns the page. Then we keep growing with Jupiter.

However, with Saturn, dreams do come true – not all of them, but some of them. Saturn is both frustration and achievement. Saturn is where we may eventually shine.

In a birth chart, Saturn shows where we will meet fear, feelings of inferiority, frustrations, obstacles and difficulties, when we will be confronted by the necessity to make choices, when we may have to put in of lot of hard work. Saturn wants us to deal with hardcore reality. Saturn shows where we are likely to feel unworthy, incompetent or inadequate. Saturn points out the big obstacles, where the big lessons are and where we may eventually reach mastery.

Saturn in a few keywords...

Achievement – Restrictions – Discipline – Frustration – Austerity – Mastery – Morality – Inhibitions – Fear – Feelings of Inadequacy – Social Status – Responsibility – Ambition – Career – Summit – Duty – Obligations – Interdictions – Form – Behaviour – Long term – Time – Structure – Control – Power – Density – Slowness – Seriousness – Ego – Superego – Contraction – Crystallization – Experience

If I kept only three words they would be:

Restriction – Structure – Ambition

Do your homework now!

8

Uranus: Expect the unexpected

Uranus, Neptune and Pluto are transpersonal planets. In the heavens, they are moving very slowly.

In a birth chart, the quicker something moves the more relevant it is in defining someone's unique personality. If you joined a group of people who were all born on the same day as you, all your planets would be in the same signs. Only your Ascendant would point at something unique about you among them.

The Ascendant – followed by the whole house system – goes around the zodiac in 24 hours. Nothing is quicker.

Imagine now that you join a group of people who were born during the same zodiacal month as you. You would have the Sun and almost all the planets in the same signs. Only your Moon and Ascendant (followed by the whole house system) would point at your unique characteristics in this group.

Uranus is a collective planet-energy. It takes eighty-four years to move through the 12 signs of the zodiac, that is seven years per sign. When you were at school, you and your classmates probably all had Uranus in the same sign, unless it was just changing sign the year you were born.

Now, suppose that something which moves quickly like the Ascendant, or perhaps a personal planet in your chart, points at Uranus by conjunction or a tight major aspect. Suddenly, this background energy comes to the fore in the makeup of your personality.

The General Principle is: the fast-moving points add value to the slower.

What is Uranus?

I defined Jupiter as a kind of Miracle Grow energy, Saturn as a crystallizing energy. Uranus is a *Shake and Change* energy. It works in three phases: build-up of tension – shake and change – new order.

With Uranus, expect the unexpected.

In nature, Uranian energy can be expressed as an earthquake or a thunderstorm. In the animal kingdom, we can see Uranus in the flight of the fly: it changes direction unexpectedly and repeatedly. It's useful to be unpredictable when birds see you as lunch.

The platypus or the okapi also look like Uranus at work. They look as if Mother Nature had gone a bit crazy and assembled parts belonging to different animals in order to make weird, new ones. You may even wonder whether extra-terrestrial beings might have experimented a bit around here before disappearing in their flying saucers. I am just illustrating the spirit of Uranus!

In the life of civilizations, Uranus brings coups and revolutions. In relationships, love at first sight or sudden break ups.

Tension, tension, tension... Shake and change! New order.

One day when Archimedes was having a bath, a metaphorical light bulb suddenly appeared above his head, and he shouted 'Eureka!' (which translates as 'I've found it!'). He would later explain that a body at rest in a fluid is acted upon by a force pushing upward which is equal to the weight of the fluid that the body displaces. Uranus is intuition, insight, breakthrough and more scientific than sentimental, especially in a bathtub with an Air sign resting in it.

Uranus, like an architect, works on the design.

When working on a plan, you draw, erase and try new things; you can change your mind in the blink of an eye.

A Uranian eccentric looks irrational, however he is more rational than average. Uranus thinks like a scientist, with a methodology which ignores irrational social codes and customs. He may well come across as the madman who has lost everything except his reason!

Uranus rules Aquarius, the sign of people who are always prepared to offer ideas. They have visions and ideals.

Voltaire (Moon in Aquarius, Uranus conjunct Ascendant) used to call God 'The Great Watchmaker'. In the spirit of Neptune, God is Love. In the spirit of Uranus, God is the Architect of the Universe, the Great Mathematician, the One who set the Sun, the planets and the stars into motion.

Love and Freedom are part of the equations.

With Uranus, the Great Mystery we are awakening to is a Universe which works like clockwork AND in which we have free will. It is paradoxical and understandable for Uranus.

By the way we have free will provided we are conscious enough to use it, so let's wake up!

It's time for a few key words:

> *Alternatives – Unexpected – Plans – Future Oriented (a plan is always about the future) – Hopes and Wishes – Abstract Thinking – Mathematics – Architecture – Freedom – Free Will – Awakening – Consciousness – Ideas and Ideals – Avant Garde – Visions*

To these we need to add:

> *Friendship – Solidarity – Community – Humanitarian Ideals – Human Society – Individuality – Originality – Rebellion – Independence – Insights – Break up – Electricity – Science – Technology*

Similar to the paradox of having Free Will in a Universe that works like clockwork is the paradox of being part of something greater than us (human communities, the human species, life, the universe) and to be at the same time absolutely unique individuals.

The process of individuation Jung talks about is what Uranus wants us to achieve: If we integrate all the different aspects of our psyche into a coherent whole, we become unique and conscious individuals, and universal at the same time.

As long as we remain unconscious, Uranus will shake us until we wake up.

Ideally, fully awakened people should not live together, conforming to social codes imposed from the outside, but according to their own inner nature. Nobody should have to betray their specialness in order to conform; everybody should cooperate freely and contribute to the common good in their own unique way.

Weirdness should be the accepted norm.

With such ideals in mind, Uranian people can come across as the most egocentric, rebellious and individualistic of all people, whilst promoting humanitarian ideals such as freedom, equality and fraternity. (The French Republic's motto)

It's Utopia or nothing. Uranian people throw spanners in the works.

Let's explore Uranus a little bit more:

If Mercury meets Shake and Change Uranus in your chart, you can't help but think differently, outside the box, and you communicate outside the box as well. The word *idiosyncrasy* was coined for you. Don't waste time wondering why not everybody gets you. If you're following your own logic rather than the ways people are used to, they won't follow you, even if your logic is more logical than their habits! Don't worry, people will agree with you eventually – maybe in the next century.

As Mercury rules studies, and Uranus is independent, you end up being self-taught, and maybe you create a new teaching style.

Mercury also rules small journeys, and Uranus likes originality, so maybe you're going from A to B walking on the roof tops or on your hands, unless you've got a monocycle... anything unusual will do.

Mercury writes and Uranus is a visionary and a social architect. Uranus-Mercury writes a manifesto.

Your nervous system is amazing. Are you always living in a state of trance?

These few examples about Uranus-Mercury are just a few examples. Life will also be larger and more creative than textbooks; that's why it's important to understand the spirit of each planet's energy.

If your Venus meets Uranus, all this nonsense in contemporary art museums, it's your fault! You are not necessarily gay. Homosexuality is just one among many possible alternatives to mainstream love.

If you have to choose between love and freedom, you can have both because you love freedom.

With Venus-Uranus you may experience love at first sight, which is the love equivalent of a Eureka moment.

Maybe you keep repeating the pattern of breaking up or being dumped suddenly and unexpectedly? This is not a curse. To break this pattern, your relationship needs to express something that will satisfy Uranus, one way or another. Be eccentric together, respect each other's freedom to be who you are and to walk off the beaten tracks. Dedicate your love to a social cause or to science like Pierre and Marie Curie...

The only revolution we need is a revolution in consciousness!

9

Longing with Neptune

Imagine. You are a river. You're going with the flow. Your ego is called *River*. There are banks on your sides. Beyond the banks, it's not you. Between the banks, it's you. It's all simple and clear.

As you flow, you grow. Sometimes there are islands in the middle of you. You become two arms that re-unite further downstream. You love the feeling!

One day, suddenly the banks disappear and you find yourself deprived of identity, swallowed by the ocean...

The consciousness that was thinking 'I am a river' panics, panics, panics... and eventually bursts out laughing. There had never been any river. There had always been water. Let there be clouds!

I introduced Jupiter as the *Miracle Grow* energy and Saturn as the crystallizing force that gives structure and form to whatever exists. In this metaphorical story, Saturn makes the banks – the limits of the temporary ego. Neptune makes them disappear.

Neptune dissolves.

Neptune connects whatever it touches to the Great Mystery.

Mystics, poets, musicians, artists, drug addicts, human wrecks and madmen are familiar with Neptune, each one in their own style.

Saviours and victims, those who sacrifice and the sacrificed, are also expressing something of this totally confusing energy.

If you had a Christian upbringing as I did, you heard that God loved the world so much that He gave His own son to be sacrificed in order to redeem humanity.

I am not discussing here whether you should believe this or not. I mention it because these are pure Neptunian themes: an absolute love, a sacrifice, a need to redeem, and we understand nothing. If God is almighty and all compassionate, why was all this necessary?

Similar themes can be found in other spiritual traditions. The necessity of a sacrifice in order to receive redemption is an archetype, a pattern in the collective psyche. Why is it there? I don't know.

With Uranus, we had an idea of God as the Great Watchmaker, the architect of the universe who has a Plan. With Neptune, God is Love. God is the Great Spirit, a being we can become intimate with. Neptune is feeling, mystic ecstasy, trance, alcoholic intoxication or the craving for it. We want to dissolve, merge, forget...

Neptune in a chart does not however, always manifest as love. Neptune dissolves. Form, structures and boundaries disappear; its effects often make us sigh: 'It's complicated!'

If Neptune is strong in your chart, you can be an empath and feel what other people are feeling as if it was your own feelings. Neptune can also take you to the psychiatric hospital, because if anything that's going on in the collective unconscious has free access to your little mind, it can literally drive you mad.

Neptune plunges you into streams of collective feelings. You may feel guilty of a collective guilt.

You can feel the trends and be the first to know what next year's fashion will be like.

You can project a fascinating image and become a star, like Marilyn Monroe. Things were certainly complicated for her, as people only saw a fantasy, not the real person behind the image.

Whether you're experiencing communion with the Divine, compassion for all beings, fascination for an inspiring but unattainable muse, possession by evil entities or psychotic disintegration, common sense doesn't apply. The ocean is pictures and feelings.

You are hypersensitive, an emotional sponge, intuitive, possibly psychic or a medium. You can be a healer, a channel or believe you're the reincarnation of Queen Cleopatra.

Sometimes, Neptune dissolves morality and willpower: you live a dissolute life. I won't go into details; I already feel tempted...

Let's summarise with a few keywords:

Dissolve – Disappear – Melt – Merge

Mystic – Communion – Love – Devotion – Hermit – Sacrifice – Feelings – Hypersensitivity – Empath – Empathy – Confusion – Illusions – Mirages – Hallucinations – Mental Health

Muse – Inspiration – Channel – Medium – Psychic skills – Healing gifts – Deception – Betrayal – Escapism – Dissolution

To understand better let's take an example. Suppose Neptune and Mercury are strongly connected in a chart.

As Mercury rules our thoughts and communication, the result can be catastrophic and the native completely confused and confusing, impervious to logic and reason, possibly dyslexic, autistic or anything similar.

The native can also be artistic, holistic and right brain rather than logical and analytical.

If Mercury finds its way through Neptune, the person can write poetry or play music.

There may also be great intuition, and the ability to be a channel and pass on messages (Mercury) from Spirit (Neptune).

Mercury is a trickster and Neptune is illusion, so this combination can amount to a talented conman. The rest of the chart will give more of an indication.

Or maybe Mercury-Neptune will manifest as a barman? Mercury rules trade, and Neptune can be alcohol. The connection with madness, addiction and the need of redemption can sometimes be expressed in something as simple as being a bartender.

As you see, there are always many possible ways to express such energies, and life will always be more diverse and abundant than all the books that will ever be written. Let's train our understanding and feel the energies! Ask Neptune, Uranus or Pluto for answers. Plug in!

I won't talk about Neptune-Venus contacts. The Romantic period is about just that. Listen to Beethoven or Schubert (who died almost as young as Amy Winehouse), cry rivers, look for your soul mate, your twin flame, your alter ego, that special one you want to be one with...

10

Under the surface and behind appearances; Pluto

Fucking Hell! ...Excuse my French, I just wanted to introduce Pluto. Profanities provide a simple and efficient way to connect emotionally with the most radical and extreme of all energies!

Pluto symbolises instincts, the power that comes from below, the sexual energy, the power in the guts. Hades, to call him by his Greek name, is the God of the Underworld. An esoteric teaching tells us that man is a microcosm. We are the universe in miniature. In our bodies, the underworld is under the belt. We feel it as guts, sex, anus. Great emotional power stems from there.

When someone says 'I am fucked' it means that they are overpowered. But if someone says 'Fuck them!' they mean 'My power first!'

'Fucking', as you know, also means 'having sex'. Isn't it a shame to use the same word to mean to mate or to abuse? Sexuality should be a sacred thing! Sex should be an act of love happening between two consenting hearts. But I am speaking like Neptune here, not like Pluto. The male spider can't help visiting the female spider on her web; if he is lucky, he won't be eaten at the end of the act, but he will have to run fast.

The energy of Neptune connects us with the myth – or nostalgia – of a lost innocence, a mythical paradise. With Neptune we want to go to heaven. Pluto is Neptune's shadow in the world of below. Pluto is the naked and unbearable truth: we are not in heaven. We are fallen angels. We have demons within. At the level of wild, unprocessed instincts, sex is not a question of love. It's power. Males fight. The winner takes it all. He gets the female, possibly a whole herd, and a territory. Pluto is ruthless.

A number of sexual fantasies and erotic games have a lot to do with overpowering or being overpowered. Would you prefer to be blindfolded and tied to the four corners of the bed, or would you prefer to do it to someone else? Pluto stages stories of power.

When human beings express Pluto's energy in its raw state, they abuse others, they commit crimes, they kill, rape and plunder like the Vikings of old on a holiday trip in Southern Europa. When civilisation fails, we hear stories of rebels displaying their enemies' heads on spikes and eating their livers to benefit from their strength. A fundamental key word is *'Archaic'* or *'Magic'*. Possibly *'Black Magic'*...

We are fascinated by Pluto. Pirates are typical Plutonian characters. Did you love Johnny Depp in *Pirates of the Caribbean*? Have you ever dreamed of flying a black flag with the skull and crossbones?

Movies are works of art and imagination. The Moon rules imagination, and Venus the arts. Let's check the natal chart of Roman Polanski. His movie 'Pirates' is such a masterpiece. Spot on! There is a Moon-Pluto-Midheaven conjunction and Venus forms a sextile to it. As you see, with a strong Pluto energy you can become a successful film director rather than become a wild beast. He was, however, convicted for sexual abuse with a minor.

In medieval times, there was a custom that allowed the feudal lord the right to sleep with a bride from his fiefdom on the night of her wedding to someone else. It was called the *'Droit de Seigneur'* and could have been called *'Pluto's right'*. Sex and power are Pluto's signature.

At the centre of our brain is a structure called the reptilian brain. Its functions are the most basic and vital. At Pluto ground level, we are still crocodiles, lizards or snakes. We are powerful and unconscious. That's scary. That's Pluto.

> *Aggression – Survival – Instincts – Fight or Flight – Territoriality – Life or Death Situations – Sexual Drive – Survival of the Individual – Survival of the Species*

That's what Pluto is about, but not only what it is about.

Before exploring further, I need to explain a little bit about how symbols work. I have introduced Pluto as an energy, whereas in fact, 'Pluto' is a symbol. What is symbolized is the raw energy I have talked about.

A symbol is a kind of 'spiritual brand'. On the material plane, a particular brand might sell for instance shoes, trousers, jackets, socks, bags, and have its own shops on the High Street. You might decide to buy something from this brand, or even work in one of their shops. A symbol is a clue. It may refer to many things.

That's why the art of interpreting an astrological chart is similar to the work of a detective. The placements of the astrological symbols are clues and it takes the talent of a Sherlock Holmes to integrate them into a coherent picture. Elementary, Doctor Watson!

Not to worry. Many basic interpretations about the placements of planets in signs and houses work well enough to be accurate in many cases. Just remember that there is much more to any symbol than the limited application of a few key words.

I started this chapter on Pluto talking about raw instincts. I could easily have started talking about *death and rebirth*, about *shamanism, mediumship* or *alchemy*, about *shit* or about *financial flows*, about *emotional welding*, about the *personal and collective unconscious* or about *evolution*. I suggest you remember these key words.

Beyond our raw instincts, Pluto also symbolises our interactions with them, what kind of lotus flowers will bloom with their roots in this mud; all the intermediate states, experiences and trials between the mud and the lotus.

When Pluto is emphasized in a chart, the individual will have psychological traits associated with the following themes: they will have *strong instincts,* be *passionate, discerning, intuitive,* maybe *psychic, able to confront extreme circumstances, possessive, fascinated by death (and possibly able to communicate with the dead), radical, strong-willed, possibly cruel or ruthless, manipulative*; unless the individual can't cope, lives *seasons in hell*, *destroys themselves*, goes through *depression* and/or needs *psychoanalysis* to confront their inner *demons*.

Sex and death have always been linked in the imagination of poets and lovers who would die for a night with each other, die in each other's arms and survive through their offspring.

Pluto, and the sign it rules, Scorpio, are also about the emotional welding of two individuals. Before Scorpio is Libra, the sign of relationships. Libra's ideal is being two. This sign emphasises the necessary compromises, the diplomacy, the good manners, the elegance we need to create harmony between partners. However, the Plutonian view is that we can't lie about who we really are when we are physically and emotionally naked in the presence of another. The Plutonian partner is perceptive, intuitive, intensely aware and ready to die in the way sperm cells and eggs die when they fuse and become a new being.

Who would waste such bliss pretending to be someone they are not? If you can't bear it, you're like Adam and Eve; with your eyes open you feel shame, you hide your nakedness behind leaves and you end up being kicked out of paradise. Plutonians are always radical. They chose the naked truth over good manners.

In our experience, death means much more than the end of our life. There are many symbolic deaths.

We can lose someone we love; *loss* is a kind of death; we say that something *dies within*...

We can also lose anything we are attached to, including our ego and our pride, which may be what we cherish most! Pluto might kill the ego and give us an *initiation*. (Another key word here!)

We become the snake who sheds its old skin. Pluto is crisis, death and rebirth. Pluto destroys the old structures and opens new creative ways. The eruption of puberty in our lives is a Plutonian phase. It happens without asking for permission – our body changes, new and intense emotions appear, and the child we once were is gone. Hormones destroy childhood.

In ethnic societies, some individuals become shamans. They have to endure difficult initiations; they confront the reality of their own death and they become able to travel to the world of spirits and negotiate with them.

With Venus and Taurus, we want to have money to ensure our material security and enjoy life. For Pluto, money is power. Whoever gets it controls the world.

Money is associated with death when we inherit it, and with emotional welding when we share our power and open a joint account. When we borrow from the bank, we borrow power. Then we are indebted; the bank has the power to take our home back if we don't pay the mortgage. The eighth house, Scorpio and Pluto speak about money when it flows, as opposed to the money we earn through our labour. When we save money and accumulate capital, it is symbolised by the second house, Venus and Taurus.

Something mysterious about symbols is that opposites coincide. Pluto symbolises the raw and wild energy and also the mystical work called *'alchemy'* which involves turning what's raw and vile into spiritual gold. Pluto is a symbol of our inner transformation.

Pluto is purification, transformation and regeneration. The raw sexual energy is but an expression of the vital force coiling like a snake at the base of the spine, the *kundalini*. Through the process of transmutation, Pluto's energies within us are called to become spiritual ideals with flesh and bones.

Power will then be handled with self-mastery.

11

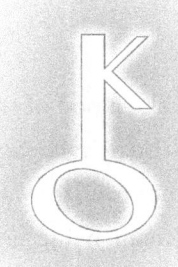

Ouch! Chiron!

Chiron, in mythology, is the wounded healer.

Mythology pushes things to the extreme, so the fact that the wound can't be cured in the myth should not scare us. Myths are stories.

When we are wounded, especially psychologically, we learn a lot; pain has always been a great motivation to try to understand what's going on. We become knowledgeable and hopefully wise. The more we try to understand, the more we know, and before we are able to sort out our own problems, we become able to understand and help those who are not as deeply hurt as we are.

The psychotherapist or healer may have great difficulties in their personal life. If they have a healthy attitude, they won't hold others responsible, they won't play victim or use all kinds of unhealthy coping mechanisms.

That's a risk on the healing path.

Much like Chiron in the myth, healers will expand their knowledge and awareness, but unlike Chiron, hopefully, will be able to heal their wounds... or at least, to "heal them enough"...

Those who are so wounded that nobody on earth can help them must find their own way, and if they find it, the wounds can themselves become blessings.

Within ourselves is our psychological home. There is a front door which can be open to others... or not. If our wounds make us close that door, we're locked inside. Our defence mechanisms become our prison.

The Great Spirit may be the only possible guest able to bring our isolation to an end and heal what needs healing, before the door can open again.

Chiron was hit in the thigh by an arrow poisoned with the blood of the Hydra, so the venom entered his own blood – surely the ultimate intimacy. 'In the thigh' may well mean in the genitals. It's certainly not too far away!

Sexuality involves the ability to approach another human being and therefore requires self-worth and acceptance, the ability to master emotions and the ability to communicate. Additionally, self-care, social skills, energy and health are also involved.

The Hydra was a monster who lived in a swamp. Its symbolism is connected with the Water element: feelings, emotions and the unconscious. Fighting the Hydra involved methods very similar to what is told in stories of vampires: in some versions, it's about stabbing the vampire through the heart – which means pointing at the core truth hiding behind layers of defence mechanisms. In other versions of the myth of Chiron, he has to drag the monster into the light – which is also a way to kill vampires, and therefore a symbol for bringing clear consciousness to whatever hides in the dark unconscious.

In order to understand particular placements, we simply need to understand what the sign, house or aspecting planets mean and what happens when wounding and healing take place at that level. We move on to this in the next chapter.

12

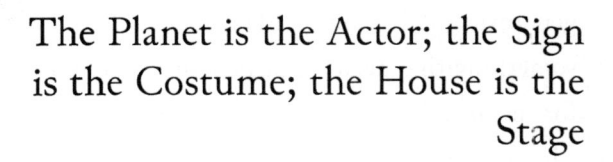

The Planet is the Actor; the Sign is the Costume; the House is the Stage

Let's get on with our visit of the astrological labyrinth.

A planet's energy is what it is before being a planet in such or such sign. If a planet was a wolf, it could be a wolf in sheep's clothing, a wolf in a tutu dress or even a naked wolf depending upon circumstances, but in all cases, it would first and foremost be a wolf. If we focus on the tutu dress and forget the animal in it, we'll miss the point. If we focus on the wolf and forget about the tutu dress, we will still miss something important, but we won't miss what's essential.

For instance, the Moon is a receptive, feminine, maternal and caring energy. She also expresses the need to be cared for, mothered, pampered, and protected. She symbolises both mother and child attitudes. Her position in the chart shows what we need to feel safe, nurtured and comfortable. Beyond these rather domestic interpretations, the Moon has also deep and wild instinctive roots. It's certainly not possible to say in a few lines what the Moon is all about. A treaty of a thousand pages would still not be enough, even though an enlightened state of consciousness could grasp it in less than one second.

For now, let's stick to the Moon as a symbol of what we need to feel safe and nurtured, and how we like to provide these things.

Let's say you have the Moon in Leo. Leo is the sign of the Sun; it is an emissive, masculine, active, creative and expressive energy. It symbolises our ego or our self and our self-expression.

Magical Doors

A Moon in Leo will still be the feminine and receptive energy the Moon essentially is; in Leo style, she will be herself with panache and generosity. Affection is likely to be publicly displayed, and is certainly something that needs to be demonstrated, but if a Leo Moon is challenged, for instance by difficult aspects, she is likely to demonstrate less desirable Moon traits in true Leo style. A person in this case may need a lot of attention and admiration to feel safe... whilst finding it difficult to give themselves and others the depth of attention they so need. They will also be unduly concerned with what other people think of them.

In this example, 'feeling cared for' is the wolf, 'seeking attention and admiration from others' is the tutu dress.

Now suppose that this wolf in a tutu dress dances in the seventh house of a birth chart. The 'house of the other' becomes the stage in this metaphor. Houses are fields of concrete experience. In the seventh house, we meet others for various purposes, like marrying them (or not getting married but living and having children together), or becoming business partners, or fighting over an issue at court, being 'open enemies' or engaging in any kind of one-to-one human interaction.

In this context, the wolf in the dress may be the person right there in front of you, showing you something you would never admit belongs to you. We are mirrors for one another and whatever we don't know and don't want to know about ourselves will appear in disguise as someone else in our lives. But that's not the only possible interpretation, as always. Maybe it's a wolf in a tutu dress that introduces you to your next significant other. Maybe it's neither you nor the other but the relationship which becomes a wolf of sorts. One way or another, the relationship field will be where this energy manifests most.

I find the notion of natural rulership really helpful. This notion is controversial nowadays. The reason is that it has been misunderstood: there is no equivalence between signs and houses, as the 'astrological alphabet'

The Planet is the Actor; the Sign is the Costume; the House is the Stage

is accused of claiming. Houses are concrete fields of experience. Signs are mindsets, or energy styles.

The twelve houses I introduce in the following chapters describe the complete cycle of earthly experience in twelve phases.

The zodiac is a cycle of twelve archetypes. It describes the archetypal core of all life cycles so it is as universal as you can get. For instance, everything that exists had at one point to get started. That's what Aries means: let there be a beginning! Aries, and Mars its ruler, naturally rule over all beginnings. And it happens that the cycle of houses begins with the first house.

The first house fundamentally means how we get started: it shows us something about how we were born, how we behave when we meet a new person, confront a new situation or initiate big or small actions. If Cancer is there, we're going to get started in Cancer style.

If the Sun is there, in Cancer, there will be powerful beginnings in Cancer style. The Dalai Lama has this placement. He doesn't look like a stereotypical Aries with his first house Sun, yet he is the leader of his people. You could say he is a Cancer doing Aries.

Astrology works with the law of analogy, which is a very ancient principle of hermetic philosophy. People who accuse the astrological alphabet of equivalence seem to forget that analogy is not equivalence. Similarity is not identity.

I

Metaphysics of the First House

I have often heard that the first house is the house of self... I would rather call it the house of the incarnated personality. What's the difference between self and personality?

It seems to me that the ultimate being at the core of everything, human, plant, animal and even mineral... is none other than the unique universal being, the Great Spirit, the Universe, Allah, the One or whatever you might want to call It. This ONE is dreaming many characters; one of these creatures is you, another is me.

There are two dimensions to the divine characters we are; a self which looks like how God dreamed us, perfect, beautiful and empty like a temple; and the incarnated personality, which is the self wrapped up in a heavy body of flesh and bones, inhabited by instincts, ancestral memories and weighted down by karma. The personality is our self – or soul – trying to express itself in the flesh, but not really succeeding yet. It's a work of clay in progress. It's a process of self-creation.

This is how I understand self and personality. If the words I'm using have different meanings for you, I hope it won't stop you from seeing the big picture. Words are but conventions.

We are Russian dolls. The smallest one at the centre is the eternal one, the same for everybody. Surrounding it is our soul, made up of many layers, like an onion.

The first house is the biggest Russian Doll. It is the house of our incarnated identity. It is the surface of our being, but it's not 'just superficial', because it is an expression of what's inside.

Etymologically, the word 'expression' means 'pressing out' and 'to exist' means 'to be outside'. The personality is expressed. The creator is at the centre.

We usually associate self-expression with the Sun and the fifth house. The Sun symbolises what is inside, what is seeking expression. The first house is how the Self is expressed by our very existence. This includes the appearance of our physical body, plus our most spontaneous attitudes and behaviour.

In the fifth house, we seek to enhance this self-expression. We want to become more like who we really are. Therefore, we create, make children, perform, paint, sing, we let our 'inner child' play around, fall in love...

Actually, there are more than just three Russian Dolls – I mentioned God, the soul and the incarnated personality. Clairvoyants describe many layers in our auras. The physical body, seen by clairvoyants, is the smallest one at the centre of wider and more subtle auric bodies. However, in the Russian dolls analogy things work the other way round, because our standard way of perceiving reality is to see the material world as being outside, and we feel the psychic and spiritual dimensions as being inside. At the centre is the heart.

As we move about in the world, we encounter, on occasion, other big Russian dolls. Sometimes what we see is what we get, and sometimes we can't guess what's inside. A limit to my metaphor is that the Russian dolls we know are identical all the way down. Inside, they all look the same.

In our reality, the challenge of manifestation is that no expression is perfect. Matter is slow and heavy. Things get a bit blurred and distorted in the process, unless we happen to be saints, enlightened masters or someone like that with a golden halo around the big doll.

Expressing our spiritual selves is a fight against density, which is Mars' job. Mars is the natural ruler of the first house. Aries, the ram, the sign ruled by Mars, is the symbol of the struggle for expression (pushing out) of the spiritual being at the centre.

All the other houses will be nothing but a series of footnotes to this first one.

Now, the ego is the idea we have about who we are but the first house is our personality. Others can see it better than we do.

We can't get off our bike to look at how we push on the pedals. We can't look at our eyes looking. Our appearance is a blind spot. We need others as mirrors, and this is what the seventh house, which opposes the first, is all about.

The first house is the house through which everything comes up. Our behaviour shows, our inner life is partially shown. Our face shows, as do our feelings, and our intentions are partially shown. Our persona shows, and what we really are is more or less shown. Our body shows, our soul is imperfectly expressed. We should believe in appearances – if only we knew how to read them without being blinded by projections and prejudices.

The Ascendant and the first house also work the other way round: we see the world and others through it, like through tinted glasses. If our Ascendant is pink, the world is pink. We all have a tendency to believe that others think or feel like us, haven't we?

(You don't like onions? How come? I LOVE onions!)

Let me add a level of complexity to the metaphor of the Russian Dolls. Imagine that all the dolls are translucent. Each doll has her own colours and motifs. At the heart/centre is the Sun, the light giver. There are a few intermediate layers. The rising sign is surface personality. What's inside shines through.

If the Ascendant is a Fire or Air sign, what comes from inside will more easily and spontaneously find its way out than if it were a more secretive Water or Earth sign. This doesn't mean that Fire or Air are better. All four elements have their role to play, and for some individuals, being less transparent is the right thing at a particular moment of their evolution. Also, if what's inside is powerfully radiant and expressive, an Earth or Water Ascendant won't prevent the outpouring.

Any planet in the first house, especially if conjunct the Ascendant, is strongly emphasised. Planets that make tight aspects to the Ascendant, especially from the 5th house, also get more immediate access to the surface of the being.

Let me suggest a meditation. The rising sign is the sign that was rising on the Eastern horizon when we were born. Its meaning is associated with the symbol of this cardinal point. East is where the Sun appears in the morning, at the end of the night. Before he was hidden, but now, a new day is dawning; a new life, full of promises, a new era!

I have tried to explain the first house as well as I can, which makes me more acutely aware of the limits of my own understanding. Symbols express deep meanings, they are the language of the Great Mystery, which is so wide and so deep! We need to deepen our understanding through reflection, daydream and meditation. We need to give these symbols time, attention and love.

14

Have your cake or eat it in the Second House

We appeared in the first house. We are now steeped in the material world, the world of duality. Welcome to the second house!

When we were born, we didn't have a sense of being a 'me', separated from the rest of the world. The rest of the world was Mother. It would take about eight months to realise that separation is even possible. When it happened, this realisation triggered great anxieties, but I'm already talking about the eighth house here, which is just opposite the second and can be seen as its shadow.

As soon as we are able to see ourselves as a separate entity it becomes possible, not only to be, but to have. The second house is the house of having.

Having is a kind of relationship. What we have is not us, but it becomes somehow an extension of us. Our 'possessive style', i.e., what we value (what we deem worth having), how we attract what we desire and how we cling to our possessions, is shown in the second house.

Venus, ruler of Taurus, the second sign, naturally rules this house.

Some people define themselves solely through their possessions. The guy with the impressive car, the platinum credit card and the dazzling blonde hanging on his arm or even the shopaholic may have forgotten that 'to be' is supposed to happen primarily in the first house and not entirely in the second.

Wisdom recommends a detached attitude towards material possessions. However, it is not possible to exist in this world without having anything at all.

When we were born, we had nothing in our pockets – in fact we didn't even have pockets, but we had a mother. She nurtured us with her milk and later on gave us food to eat and clothes to wear, her constant presence and all kinds of things became ours. Our teddy bear, our bed, our room, our toys, our shoes, our plate. Hopefully we had a Dad too.

Throughout life, we will have things and people. I should rather say *attachments*. The second house is unavoidable.

Before eating our cake, we must have it. It goes the same way with jacket potatoes or vegan pastas. Once eaten, the food becomes part of us. We will go to the loo in the eighth house of letting go, but for now, in the second, we are just adding to who we are by having more.

We will apply this fundamental pattern of having and adding to ourselves over a wide-ranging field, on different levels and in different styles. It will all be symbolised by this house.

How many different ways can there be to have a cake and eat it?

You can take your time or eat it as quickly as possible lest someone else grabs it and eats it instead of you; you can start with the icing – if you consider the icing to be the best bit – or keep it for the end; you can munch slowly and enjoy it sensually, or stuff yourself with as much as possible, just to feel full because it makes you feel safe; you can eat it with your fingers or have manners and use a little spoon elegantly; you can eat a cake you've baked yourself or only eat cake when someone makes one for you; you can share it or save it for later; you can eat a cake you don't really like just because everyone says this cake is the best you can get; you can sit outside for everyone to see what you're eating and envy you; you can decide that you are above something as trivial as eating cake and pretend you don't care. I leave it to you to connect these different cake eating styles with zodiacal signs and imagine other situations. It's all a second house story.

Notice here that cake is more than just food; it is pleasure as well.

Traditionally, the second house is the house of earning money. Money stands for all the things we can have, all the things we may need or desire,

Have your cake or eat it in the Second House

all the things we value. The second house is the house of values. Values are not only material, but also emotional, mental and spiritual. Having a lover is having emotional food on our plate. We want to eat a lover; at a subtle level of energy, we really do. We absorb their vibes, breathe in their odour, we are hungry for them and them for us. I am not saying that the second house is the house of love, (it's traditionally the fifth), but that this 'eating each other' dimension of love pertains to the second house.

What is better than being valued by someone we value to the point of making love together?

Being desired is good for our self-esteem, but we need a little bit of self-esteem for this to happen in the first place.

The second house is also about self-esteem. The more we attribute value to things and people the more we are likely to wonder about our own value. Are we worth having as a daughter or a son? What may our parents' point of view be? What do we feel about that? Are we worth having as a friend at school? Are we worth having as a collaborator, as a business partner, as a lover, as a mother, as a father…? Concretely, do we have value? Most probably, yes. Now, what kind of value do we have?

All the people we have in our lives feed us with their particular way of being. We feed them in return with our own energies. We get attached. The second house is the house of attachments.

The seventh house, the other house ruled by Venus, is said to be the house of partnerships. The meanings definitely overlap.

Who is worth getting attached to? The beautiful, the compassionate, the funny, the adventurer, the listener, the sweet, the kind, the strong, the clever, the skilful, the reliable, the spiritual…? It depends on what we value more. What do we want? What would we buy if we won the lottery?

Our relationship with our body is ambiguous. We talk about it as something we possess (my legs, my nose, my butt, my nostrils, my body), whilst simultaneously identifying with it.

In the first house, the body is an expression of who we are. In the second, it's our most precious possession – the second house says something about our relationship with our body, and our body is our connection to nature... Do we owe the earth or does the earth owe us?

Following this thread, one interpretation of Jupiter in the second house may be that we are going to be attracted by a kind of faith (Jupiter) connected with nature, like paganism or animism. Something that values the body as a temple of spirit. Unless this Jupiter suffers from serious afflictions, in which case the flesh may be considered guilty, shameful or perverted.

To consider the different aspects of a problem, we can ask the fundamental questions: *What? How? Why? Who?*

When we apply the question *How?* to the content of the second house, we learn something about how we manage to get into our lives the things or people we value.

The second house is also called the house of inner resources. What do we have within ourselves that will enable us to get what we need and desire?

In conclusion, the principle of the second house is extremely simple: it is *to have*.

Money – self-esteem – value – values – body – inner resources – are all essential key words.

This house is also as complex and varied in its expressions as life itself. We can have material goods, people, skills, gifts, qualities. We can have and be had. What we own owns us. We get attached. Without attachments, we wouldn't be incarnated.

Let's keep our beginners' spirit open, the study of astrology is an ongoing meditation...

15

Magic in the Third House

In the first house we simply are, like the biggest in a series of Russian dolls, showing up in the here and now! First is Fire, that creative impulse happening as if out of nowhere.

In the second house we become flesh. We suckle, we incorporate, we absorb, we possess, we have... the second is Earth. We become substance.

In the third house we start asking questions. We now have big eyes, trying to seize the world as if its colours and shapes could be eaten from a distance. In some way, they can be. We absorb our environment; we take it all in!

Our ears absorb sounds which the mouth will try to reproduce. The first words will be 'Mum' and 'Dad'.

Maybe one day we will go to the ninth house, the house of higher learning, and study linguistics. We will learn about the *signifier* and the *signified*. The signifier is the sound 'Mum' and the signified is the actual Mum. There is a relationship between the two.

In the third house, we are learning our first language. As soon as we can say 'Mum' it becomes possible to call her when she is looking away, and speak about her in her absence.

From then on, we will live in two parallel worlds, which ideally should be twins: the map and the territory. The world of language will echo the world we touch, hear, feel, see, experiment. In case of discrepancies, we will get anxious or laugh at the good joke! It is now also possible to lie.

From now on these two worlds will drift apart. A whole new life will colonise the new world. Talking becomes a universe in its own right: it is how human beings relate to one another.

At the same time, we keep exploring, walking on our hands and knees, and on our two legs; we grab things and put them into our mouths, we grab words and usher them out. We become mobile, deft, skilled, able to run away, able to climb, to crawl, to hide, to move, to laugh at peek-a-boo!

The third house is an Air house, an analogy of Gemini, sign of the twins, and with it we learn to live from a distance. In our environment, there are things and people. Mum, Dad and others. Siblings. The neighbours' children. Schoolmates. At school we will keep perfecting our knowledge of the intellectual map of the world. Reading, writing, counting, reasoning, learning by heart, reciting...

Life is a school, that's why I think schools shouldn't take up too much time in the life of children. We imitate, imitate, imitate... Imitating is knowing, little monkeys! That's how we learn.

Can you walk on your hands? Can you pass the ball? Can you ride a bicycle? Can you hit the target? Can you climb trees? Look at how I'm doing!

The psychologist Piaget, in his theory of cognitive development, called the first stage the sensorimotor stage, which means experimenting through our senses and movements. These are the first steps on the route towards knowledge. They consist of experimenting with life through our senses as babies do. For instance, we wouldn't have any idea of what "hard" means if we never touched anything hard.

In the universe of language, children know a magic formula which protects them against the spells that others sometimes cast on them: if someone says you are ugly or stupid, don't let the label stick onto your fledgling, sensitive self-esteem. Just answer:

What you say is what you are!

This protection is very important, because, 'As we speak, we create!'

The world of language doesn't passively reflect the objective world of experience; it is now taking control, shaping whatever is beyond objectivity.

What is beautiful? What is ugly? Who is clever? Who is stupid? Answer: Whoever or whatever is said to be so.

The power of words and thoughts is so great that we believe in the power of making things appear and disappear in the universe of things with the power of incantations and magic formulas. And it's even true... *to some extent*!

If we hold the two parallel worlds together with integrity, walking the talk and talking the walk so as to keep the twin worlds neatly intertwined, our words will have the greatest power.

Sometimes we say that Mercury – ruler of Gemini, natural ruler of this third house – represents the mind. In my view, it represents the side of the mind which uses words and language; the Mercury mind names, talks, communicates and reasons logically.

The mind is also symbolised by the Moon: daydreaming, dreaming, feeling moved, using our imagination or conjuring up memories – all are happening in our minds. Jupiter represents the mind as well, especially when it works in a holistic way and confronts the great philosophical and religious questions which require our mental faculties to stretch beyond common sense, logic and everyday language.

The Self came up in the first house, then added to itself by eating and possessing in the second house. It is now interacting with the environment in the third house. Here we move, here we speak, here we meet peers, brothers and sisters, neighbours, schoolmates; here we imitate, learn, reason, think, communicate... The self that expresses itself from within, the biggest of the Russian dolls, is now shaped from outside.

As it interacts it has to adapt to the environment. All the smaller Russian dolls within have to adjust as the process moves along.

IV

16

Secrets of the Fourth House

Where are you from? Where do you belong? How about your emotional foundations?

I introduced the first house as being the house of the incarnated self and illustrated this with the symbol of the Russian dolls: the smallest doll, at the centre, is the spiritual being; the biggest one, created in the image and likeness of the central one meets the outer world.

I didn't mention an important detail. The biggest doll has drunk the waters of oblivion from the Lethe River. Our bodies and our behavioural patterns may be expressing the truth of who we really are at the core, but we have forgotten this fact. We don't know who on earth we might be!

We are now living in the world of reflections. The Moon is Queen. Matter is Mother. We receive from her not only our body, shaped in her womb, but everything we need for our survival and well-being. Her breast is the great provider. Her attention is our guarantee of existence. Around her is a house, a closed and warm space that's a little bit like a bigger womb, and maybe there is a father, a husband who provides for her as she provides for us. Or maybe there is no father, no husband, but a family nevertheless, grandparents, uncles and aunts, there is always another layer of protective and nurturing cocoon around us and mother... or at least there should be.

Around our family, there may be a village, a city, a nation, possibly a welfare state contributing to the security and protection of mothers and babies; they wrote our name on their registers as soon as we were born.

There is also a culture surrounding us. Maybe we were baptised or went through some other ritual involving water or earth, meaning that we belonged where we belonged.

We belong to this earth; we live within the lunar orbit.

As above, so below. The Moon reflects the realities of the spiritual world. In the water, images are inverted. In the fourth house, we can still think of our existence as a set of Russian dolls, like in the first house, but we are now the smallest one at the centre; from this point of view, we don't express our being from inside out, we are now impressed upon from outside in. We receive all influences from all directions, and we are incredibly sensitive. Maybe everything that comes to us from this outside world is the lunar echo of what we are within, but we don't know that.

Maybe one day we will study astrology, think poetically, wonder about esoteric laws and suspect that everything is only one thing!

The fourth house is the house of our emotional foundations. If a baby feels safe and welcome, he or she is likely to feel so for life. All the impressions of childhood shape our attitudes, our emotions and feelings, our sense of who we are. Without knowing it, we are our parents, our grandparents, our ancestors, the earth they walked on, the sacred place where they are buried; we are what they lived, we are their continuation, we are history.

When the fourth house is activated in a chart, some of the themes associated with it will manifest, whether in our minds, our souls or as events.

Someone with the Sun (or any planet related to career) in the fourth house can become an estate agent and make a living buying and selling properties: it is fourth house business as we grow up in homes. Yes, sometimes interpretations can be as basic as that.

Working from home is another interpretation of an indicator of career in this house (if you have Saturn or the ruler of the tenth house in the fourth for instance). If this indicator is Mars, it could also mean being a soldier – a warrior dedicated to protect the motherland.

Whether related to career or not, another expression of the fourth house can be an interest in history and anything related to our origins, to the past, to our ancestors and traditions. The historian, the storyteller, the West African griot, the genealogist, the archaeologist – all have business in the fourth house. We are the harvest of the past. Knowing the past is knowing who we are. Where do we come from? Were we once apes jumping from branch to branch high up in the trees?

Indicators of knowledge (Mercury, Jupiter, the rulers of the third and ninth house) in the fourth house will turn our interests toward the past.

Our origins are not only collective. Our personal origin is our mother, and also our father indeed. We have received our genes from them, half from one, half from the other. Traditional astrologers say that the fourth house represents the father and the tenth, the mother. Modern astrologers associate houses and signs. As the 4th sign is Cancer, ruled by the Moon, it's difficult not to see mother in it. I'm pretty sure it's half-half, like in our DNA!

We also receive a whole package of emotional patterns from our family, which may one day lead us into the office of another fourth house worker: the psychologist, or the psychogenealogist. These professions are actually connected with all three watery houses. Exploring the past is more specifically fourth house-minded. As children, we felt before we thought. We imagined and dreamt before we reasoned. We were sensitive before being logical... and we still are!

The fourth house is a most private and intimate house. If you have ever done a guided meditation with a hypnotherapist, maybe you were told to imagine you were descending a long, winding staircase deep within the earth. At the bottom of the stairs, there was a door, and behind this door, a secret room – your secret place, your secret garden (if you prefer it to be a garden). There you are absolutely safe and protected. This inner world is your fourth house.

Nobody has ever been as close to you as your mother was.

17

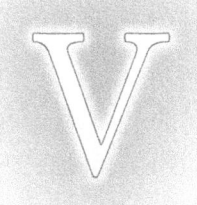

The show must go on in the Fifth House

As an introduction to the fifth house, let me light a firework. The rocket will shoot upwards at high speed; I associate this phase with the first house. The energy is like Mars, strong, focused, hurtling towards a goal. At the top of its trajectory the firework bursts like a flower. The spectators cheer. Now the energy is like the Sun, majestic, expressing itself outwards from the centre in all directions... We are in the fifth house.

The fifth house is associated with the Fire element. It is a succedent house. Let me explain some generalities:

There are four angles in a chart, the Ascendant, the MC, or Midheaven (the highest point a planet can reach in its course through the sky), the Descendant, opposite the Ascendant, and the IC, opposite the Midheaven.

The four 'angular' houses (1st, 4th, 7th and 10th) start with the Ascendant. Traditionally, they are considered the most important houses. I disagree with the notion that some houses are more important and other less so. However, if we consider that traditionally the first house is the house of self; the fourth the house of home and family; the seventh the house of relationships and the tenth the house of career, we can then accept them as representing the 'pillars' of human life.

A key word for angular houses is *Action*.

The succedent houses (2nd, 5th, 8th and 11th) come after the angular ones. They are traditionally considered less powerful. A key word for them could be *stability* or *desire for stability*. Stephen Arroyo says *security*.

Using fireworks as a metaphor, it's easy to understand: action is taken when the rocket is shot towards the sky, and when it bursts, we live in the

71

present moment, enjoying the outcome. Fireworks don't last for very long, but compared to a rocket shooting upwards, there is a relative stability. The state of tension towards a goal is over when the goal is reached.

Again, when I explained the first house, I used the metaphor of the Russian dolls. At the core is spiritual reality, symbolized by the smallest doll. The biggest doll is the outward expression of inner reality. However, it is an imperfect expression.

The first house shows how we approach reality in an immediate way. We don't rehearse in this house. If life is a stage, we are characters in the play from the moment we are born.

However, not everything that exists within reaches the surface and not everything that reaches the surface does so in the most brilliant way.

When we are in the fifth house, we want to express more of ourselves than just our everyday life persona. In the fifth, we want our whole Self, our healed Self to shine through. We are like the rocket shooting upwards saying: 'Wait! There is more to me than that!'

The fifth house is the house of the Sun. That's the reason why I disagree with the notion that angular houses are the most powerful. It seems to me that the house of the Sun can't be seen as weaker, or of lesser importance, than the house of Mars. However, it can make sense to think that when you let off a rocket, the most powerful moment is when it is shooting upwards.

The zodiac and its symbols can be seen through many lenses.

After the succedent houses come the cadent houses, traditionally considered the weakest ones. They are the third, sixth, ninth and twelfth houses. A key word for them is *Learning*. Maybe they are outwardly weaker but inwardly stronger. The most spiritually oriented houses, the ninth and the twelfth, are cadent houses. Spirituality may well be humanity's weakest point, it doesn't have to be!

The show must go on in the Fifth House

Let's go back to the fifth house. I was surprised when I was a beginner to find this house (naturally ruled by the Sun, symbol of kingship, power and brilliance), is called the house of fun and entertainment.

Traditional astrology offers us a list of interpretations for every house, but it doesn't say what makes all these meanings coherent. For the fifth, you get: *love life – pleasures – children – education – artistic achievements – games and sports – haphazard gains – speculations and clothing.*

Even with *self-expression* on your mind, the common thread between the above elements of this list is not obvious! Keep this list in mind and follow me through some philosophical musings...

I loved listening to the philosopher Alan Watts explaining that the purpose of life is no more about reaching a goal than the purpose of a piece of music is to reach its end. The pleasure of listening to a piece of music is felt as the music is playing. Life, if created by a Great Spirit, (eternal, absolute and needing absolutely nothing), can only be a work of art, a creation.

Love then is the only reason.

Suffering may be part of life, but suffering is only intolerable when we are blinded by illusions. In reality, like in art, there are only tensions and resolutions. If we reach the level of consciousness in which we can dissipate the illusions, suffering will disappear, we will enter nirvana and see: life is a ballet. It's a game. It's a piece of music, a theatre, a movie... The show must go on!

When we create, we show who we are because we are creators.

We were created in the image of the Creator, weren't we?

When we are having fun, when we play like children, we live for the sake of the present moment; when we are in love and love is reciprocated, all we love is what is.

Love only happens between authentic selves; authentic selves need to be expressed, to be seen and loved, and when it happens, lovers play with each other. Courtship is a love game. In such moments, life doesn't need a meaning. Life says *I am this*, if it says it in Sanskrit it says '*Soham*', if it takes the appearance of a burning bush it says *'I am that I am'*.

There is no other meaning to life than life, and life is the Great Spirit's work of art, woven with love (because if he didn't love it, the Great Spirit wouldn't have done it, don't you think?)

We are the Great Spirit's children, and like the Great Spirit, we are creators and we have children. Our children are our creations, and conversely, when we create something, we say: '*It's my baby!*' (creating goes beyond creating works of art. We can create a business, a social event, build a house, design a garden, whatever...)

Educating children involves being a role model. It's a show and it had better be good! We lead by example. We show who we are. The house of learning is the third house. Education is the fifth. If we confuse teaching how to read, write, count and when William the Conqueror won the battle of Hastings with education, we are sadly mistaken.

Now of course there are things children should learn. It happens that the best way to learn is to play. Maria Montessori had incredible results with small children. Four- or five-year-olds would learn how to read in three months, without being pressured to do any work. They had letters to play with, and grown-ups willing to *show* them what they wanted to know. You've certainly experienced that yourself: when you are having fun doing something, you learn incredibly quickly. You ask someone to show you, you get it, you enjoy!

The connection between clothing and showing is quite obvious. The first house says something about our physical body among other things. We appear with a certain face and body type. In the fifth we can be creative, put on makeup, chose a style...

Love, romance, pleasures, shows, art, fun, children, education, clothing... I think I have listed almost all the main themes. I didn't mention *speculation* and *haphazard gains*. They are games.

The show must go on in the Fifth House

Being born with a Sun-Neptune conjunction in this house, let me tell you: making life a work of art is an ideal. It is on the horizon. We are heading in that direction. Our ultimate destination is the Sun, away from the shadows.

VI

18

The witch's broom is in the Sixth House

When we were small children, we didn't know much about this brand-new world in which we had just arrived. We would learn how to do all sorts of things with our bodies: moving, touching, grabbing, holding, crawling, putting objects into our mouth, walking on our hands and knees.

Have you ever seen a baby dropping an object and being so amazed watching it fall? It was not obvious that things fall at that age. It was quite a discovery!

We were complete beginners. Before we learned, we didn't even know that something that our mother would hide from us carried on existing somewhere out of sight!

As we became more acquainted with the ways of this world, we built mental representations of it. We became able to hold the memory of the Teddy Bear in our mind and look for it. (This is called *Object Permanence* in cognitive development.)

In the sixth house, analogous to Virgo, we learn the material world, we experiment with our bodies and we build our minds in the process.

A long time later we will have built a useful mind for everyday activity, with a whole lot of mental scripts about how things work and how to deal with them.

As adults if we pick up a broom, we know how to handle it. If we go to the restaurant, we follow a sequence of actions: pushing the door, walking in, being welcomed by a waiter and asked 'how many people?', being shown where to sit, reading the menu... It's all easy because we are following a *script*. We started with things falling and objects being permanent, and here we are, ordering food without Mum's help, thanks to a well-functioning mind.

If we had never been to a restaurant before, it would be an adventure; we would not know how to behave and would have to figure it all out. We would feel anxious or excited. We would look stupid or embarrassed. We would hesitate, ask weird questions... as we do in the ninth house when we visit another culture and don't know the customs.

We have mental scripts for everything we do. A professional is someone who has acquired precise mental patterns about how to deal with a specific kind of activity, like repairing the central heating. They also have the necessary tools at hand. When you wonder what kind of work is best suited to the person whose chart you're reading, look at the sixth house. What are their habits? We don't see directly the habits in the chart, but we see combinations of symbols: a sign, possibly with planets in it. When it comes to the sixth house, these symbols represent mental patterns that will manifest as a certain style of habits. This style can tell us something about what kind of work suits them. For example, Venus in Pisces in the sixth house may manifest as the habit of indulging in eating, drinking and sleeping a bit too much, but Venus in Pisces could also be very agreeable and empathetic in work like being a receptionist. We may not think of work as a receptionist if we consider that someone is a bit overindulgent, but we may think of it from Venus in Pisces...

Our daily routines follow the same principles. Books with titles like *Seven Habits of Successful People* could be re-titled: 'Successful settings for your sixth house'. Good habits are very powerful because once a script is written in the mind, we don't need much energy and attention to repeat it day after day. We run on automatic pilot and things get done.

For instance, if you're used to putting your coat on a hanger each time you come back home, it doesn't cost you much energy to do it. If your new partner hasn't this script set up in their mind, you are likely to keep getting irritated by him for a long time. You may tell him: 'For God's sake, it's not

The witch's broom is in the Sixth House

difficult to put your coat on a hanger and your dirty socks in the laundry! Please keep our house tidy!' In your experience, it's not difficult. But for your partner, it is. To change his habit of dropping his clothes wherever they fall, he will have to remember to bring his conscious attention to what he is doing in the present moment, stop following his usual script (taking clothes off – dropping them – grabbing a beer). Not following the usual script creates discomfort; our brains want repetition. He will have to consciously hang his coat on the hanger, which, I admit, is not such a big deal, however it will be necessary to repeat the conscious behaviour a number of times before it becomes natural, and after the coat it will be the socks, after the socks, the bed, the broom, the cooking, the shopping, the cleaning, the paperwork... It may become overwhelming for someone who has not acquired all these good habits to set up all these new mental scripts whilst their partner may not even acknowledge the real effort of mental reprogramming. A well-functioning sixth is good for the seventh!

I read somewhere that in Roman times, the sixth house was the house associated with slavery. It makes sense. A slave does what they are told to do. Whether what they are doing is good or bad, right or wrong is none of their business, they are serving a master, no more no less. The sixth house serves you. It's your own inner slave. Let's say your *inner servant.*

By extension, the sixth house rules relations between employers and employees, between superiors and inferiors, and also includes our relations with our pets. For information about your cats and dogs, look at the sixth house!

Do you know the story of the Sorcerer's Apprentice? It's from German folklore. Goethe wrote a poem about it, Paul Dukas composed the music and Mickey Mouse plays the role in Walt Disney's *Fantasia*. It's a pure sixth house story.

The sorcerer's apprentice has a lot of chores to perform, in particular drawing water from a well. He enchants a broom to do the work for him, but the broom, like an efficient sixth house script, keeps doing the job again and again. The apprentice chops the broom in many pieces in an attempt to stop it, but then all the pieces become brooms and keep fetching water again and again until the master sorcerer comes back and stops it all.

Our habits have the power of these brooms. In the long term, they can make us rich or ruin our health; if not mastered with consciousness and a bit of will power, we become their victims. We move in with someone we love and we end up with a relationship disintegrating over domestic disputes about socks and laundry.

The sixth house is the house of magic. A ritual is a script: a series of actions accompanied with words in a specific order. Every detail counts. If magic is, as I believe, the art of giving precise orders to our minds, a ritual starts at a fundamental level with material elements and our bodies. How our minds may command the situation can be as simple as a modification of our daily habits, or as mysterious as any manifestation of the unconscious, or maybe the spiritual world gets involved. Who knows?

As the proverb goes:

God helps those that help themselves.

Now, if we say prayers or utter positive affirmations whilst sending different signals through the way we behave, the results we'll get will be in accordance with our attitudes. Our first language is the language of what we are doing and how. Magic begins with the way we hold the broom.

I once had the opportunity to look at the chart of a rabbi. I think this guy was really meant to be a rabbi. The Moon was on the MC – the Moon means mother, family and where we belong. To be Jewish is passed on by the mother. He had the Sun in the sixth house. I asked him if he performed a lot of rituals, and of course he did. Mind, body, spirit.

Our daily routines include both what we eat day after day and how we eat it, and this indeed has an influence on our health. Our body is the basis of our experience of life, it supports our mind. Here again there are patterns, rhythms, cycles. Fortunately we are not conscious of it all. Our metabolism happens without our meddling. Our mind is a baby compared to the complexity of all our bodily functions. As we evolve, we will have to expand our consciousness within as well. Let's start with a little relaxation. Relax the muscles, listen to your breath. Life is not only all about the patterns of the outside world…

To end this chapter, I would like to mention another thread of meditation: the common root of the words *'organic', 'organs', 'organism'* and *'organisation'* is the Greek word *'organon'* meaning *'tool'*.

In an organism, for instance in our body, there are many specialised parts, each performing a particular function in the service of the whole. Health is when every part works well. A human society is an organism. Everyone contributes through their work. In a healthy society, wealth is created by all and fairly redistributed to all.

Astrology, nevertheless, doesn't say whether communism is better than capitalism though. In my view, it's more a question of state of mind than political structures.

In an organic society everyone works as a service to the whole, and as a result of working well, every part benefits from the health of the whole.

Service is the healthy mindset.

VII

19

Once upon a time in the Seventh House

If you say *relationship* to an astrologer, they will look straightaway at the *'House of the Other'*.

Placements in the seventh house often seem to more accurately describe your partner(s) than yourself. However, whatever happens in our seventh house is still happening in our own chart!

You must know the story of the ugly duckling. The poor little bird is a survivor. He doesn't know he is a swan. He believes he is a duck, and an ugly one. However, when he sees the swans, he is fascinated by them.

When the swans see the ugly duckling, they see a swan. They approach him. They make him look at his reflection in the water... and...Surprise! He is a swan!

Others are mirrors. Is this mirror reliable? Sometimes yes and sometimes no. Apologies for the Libran answer to that question. Maybe. To some extent. We need a sense of nuances. We are not on solid ground here...

Can we tell a woman who is a victim of domestic abuse or sexual violence that she is herself a tormentor who doesn't know herself, like in the ugly duckling story but the other way round? This would be a horrible thing to say! So, let's accept that things may be a little bit more complicated.

Freud wrote that people without moral standards never develop neurosis. They follow their impulses and they don't end up in the therapist's room. Those people don't have a little red devil on one shoulder and a little white angel on the other, arguing about how they should behave. They only have the little red devil. No inner conflict, no neurosis.

The little red devil is not evil. He is just the voice of a less evolved version of us. If you put a piece of meat between two dogs, they are likely to fight. They are not evil; they are just dogs. They are lovely. They don't have a little angelic dog on their shoulder telling them they should sacrifice themselves and let the other dog have the meat.

The seventh house is where our inner dogs (or whatever our spirit animals may be) sign a social contract. We understand that life can only be better if we refrain from behaving like we were in a *'state of nature'* and strive for fairness instead. The purpose is to keep the peace with minimum suffering and maximum happiness for everyone.

Imagine the two dogs in my example. They have agreed that constant fighting gets them nowhere. Now they argue instead. The smaller one thinks that a fair share of a piece of meat is a fifty-fifty split, whilst the bigger one claims that fairness consists of awarding each a piece that's proportionate to their size – or to their weight. Which is fairer? Sharing in proportion of weight or size?

From now on it will always be possible to split more hairs. The archetype behind the seventh house is Libra.

Civilised beings go to court instead of fighting. The seventh house also means lawsuits and court cases. (Woof! Woof! That's not fair, Your Honour! I'm twice as big, I should get more meat!)

When we get married or go into business with an associate, we sign a contract. We want win-win situations. It all happens in the magnificent seventh house.

When we engage in relationships however, we don't discuss all the terms and conditions in advance. Should we? The magic of love may not feel so good if we did.

What is fair? In a relationship, should we always tell our significant other where we are going and when we will be back?

Should partners do the same amount of housework regardless of how much money they contribute?

If the relationship is a friendship, should the friends be willing to answer the phone or open their door at any time of the day or night if requested?

(Some friendships are one to one partnerships in their own right.)

Psychological questions, emotional needs and desires are at stake. If put in writing, the unspoken contracts that partners unconsciously agree on might look like:

Make me feel safe and I will make you feel special

Boost my ego and I'll boost yours

Bring some structure, I'll provide emotional intelligence

I'll make you laugh and you'll help me cope with the sad bits

I will hit you. This will relieve your in-built guilt and my inner tensions ...

All kinds of unspoken contracts can exist, but I have a feeling that we are already entering the eighth house... Real life is not as clearly compartmentalised as in a birth chart. In the seventh house we engage in relationships, in the eighth we deal with the deep emotional stuff. In the ninth, we'll try to understand the meaning of life.

At the beginning of this chapter, I mentioned the law of attraction: *'Like attracts like'*. I'm taking issue with the universality of this principle. It seems to me that we can also attract (and feel attracted to) opposites. If like attracted like and like only, we would all be gay, wouldn't we?

Reality must be more nuanced.

Let's go back to having that little red demon on one shoulder and the angel on the other. Imagine a woman who is very scared by the little demon. She gives maximum attention and power to the angel, she listens only to the voice who talks about tolerating, sharing, giving, self-sacrificing... She doesn't realise that this angel is not a real angel. It's just a voice dressed up as one. This voice alone is not fair. The symbol of balance, the scales, must have two sides. The little red demon, spokesman for personal desires and needs is oppressed, suppressed and this is inner abuse. Self-abuse.

In true seventh house logic, this inner abuse is likely to manifest as abuse coming from outside. In this way, yes, like attracts like...

Why is this woman so scared by her little demon who only wants her to survive, have some pleasure and be happy? Maybe that's her karma. I must stress: MAYBE, she let him talk too loudly in some past life, many thousands of years ago, while the angel was the oppressed and suppressed one, and now, her karma is that the scales have tipped. She is abusing herself within and therefore attracts abuse from the outside world. Maybe.

But MAYBE it is down to great generosity that she has taken on a part of someone's suffering, not because of karma but because of a will to take some of the pain of another upon her own shoulders and contribute to healing it. If Christians believe that Jesus took the sins of the world upon himself, then why might someone else not share the burden of another?

And maybe... maybe something else.

All I want to say here is that we can't judge because we can't know. One way or another the seventh is a mirror, but this should not be taken too simplistically.

Sometimes we need to know we are a swan. Sometimes we need to rectify something within ourselves, which can be similar, or opposite to what is presented to us by a partner.

In a mirror, your left side becomes your reflection's right side and vice versa.

When we look at someone, we see two people in them: one is us, the other is them. When we know who we are, we know who they are...

VIII

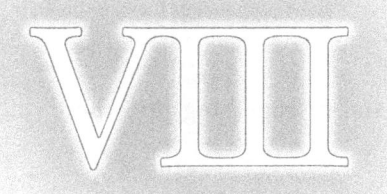

20

Death in the Eighth House

The eighth house is full of scary monsters: death, sex, power, ghosts and rivers of money. Once you've been sucked into this house, only one thing is certain: nothing will ever be the same again.

How could it be? This is the House of Transformation.

An archetypal expression of the eighth house is puberty.

You didn't have hair sprouting out all over the place. You didn't have breasts or periods. If you were a boy your voice was still high pitched. Your body was a child's body.

You had a variety of interests, you were quite spontaneous, you didn't mind being silly now and again (or even all the time), and suddenly, as abruptly as Hades opening the earth under Persephone's feet, the hormones shouted: *Game over!*

Maybe it was not as sudden as I, (a male Scorpio with the eighth house in Aquarius) claim it to be. It could have happened more gradually, but inexorably anyway.

Some time later, you looked at a picture of yourself taken a few years earlier and you thought: *'This was me!'*

It felt weird.

Did you feel regret? Did you realize that you were facing your own death as you looked at this child who was no more? When did you realize for the first time that life was not forever?

In the meantime, you were so excited and scared. You were experimenting with your powers of attraction and seduction!

Where was your place in the new game? Were you highly ranked, followed, sought after? Did you dare to show off your brand new 'me'?

Did you feel better off dressing up as a flower and disappearing into the wallpaper?

This was a ruthless game for sure. Not everyone was valued equally. Sexual attractiveness knows no political correctness. Cruelty happens. You could win one day and be dumped the next. Drama was everywhere...

Do you remember? Or has the teenager you once were been buried in the depths of your forgotten memories along with the child?

You will die as well. Each time you put a foot or a finger in the eighth house, something dies, but something new springs up. Death is not the end of life, you know! The feelings are intense and the uncertainty certain. Sometimes it is wonderful, like a new love disturbing all the plans and the daily routines. Sometimes there are rivers of tears going down the drain. Nothing can ever be the same after passing through the house of transformation.

The eighth house pattern applies to all the in-between times.

This is not an everyday house like the sixth. You don't wake up every morning with some eighth house business to go about. We die a little bit every day, but we don't notice all the time. It's an underground program.

The eight house follows the seventh. So, you have found a partner. A good candidate for the long term. One day you find yourselves living in the same space. Your life as an independent single being has definitely come to an end. Now, with your new partner, you've got sex and bills. You share your resources. You both put your books on the same shelves. You hang your pictures, posters and paintings next to one another on the same walls. Together you count up what you can afford. In the bedroom you exchange bodily fluids, mix your dreams and blend your energies. You see each other naked, both physically and emotionally. If you don't, it didn't work as it should have. Intimacy is sharing what usually remains hidden and that's how you become one.

Another eighth house crisis may one day give you your freedom back, but for now, you are creating a new unit, and in the process, you may lose big chunks of what you assumed was your personal identity.

In the eighth, the ego dies.

There are other transformations in a human life, some are big and others small.

There are also rivers of money in the eighth house. In the second, we acquire, we accumulate, we save. Big second house money becomes capital. In the eighth house, money flows.

The eighth is a Water house and money is liquid. Sometimes it flows in and sometimes it flows out.

Sometimes you get some on the way back from the graveyard, along with some communication from the other world. Sometimes someone you once loved to the point of having children with them makes you pay, emotionally and financially. Sometimes you go to the bank to borrow some power. Sometimes you pay, or get paid for sex. (Not you, dear reader, another reader).

Money is value. Money becomes a symbol of value. Emotions are attached to whatever is valued and emotions flow like money, they can be shared like money and they have power. Symbolic logic is a strange logic!

We only have to observe life to see how its threads are intertwined. Death (and the other world, and the occult), sex, power, money, transformation...

When we interpret an eighth house placement, we don't always need to come up with the whole Shakespearean drama. In many cases, only something associated with these themes and emotional storms will be relevant, thank God!

21

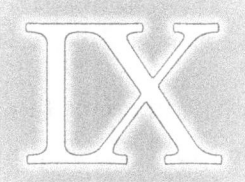

Seeking for the truth of the Ninth House

In the big wide world, there are quite a few people who are very keen to give you good advice about how to create the life of your dreams.

They claim to know THE secret. They want to tell you about the laws of the Universe. They claim to know how to 'manifest' anything: love, money, health...

Such people appear for the sake of the ninth house indeed. Not as its best expression, but let's take it from there.

The human condition is such that we don't really know what life is and how it works, however, we want to understand. We want to be able to suffer less and live a happy and fulfilled life instead.

We become truth seekers. We want the fountain of immortality. We want to find the Grail!

We want to know about reality and how to deal with it.

We're ready to travel to the end of the world to find out.

I won't talk much about travels here, so I'll just quickly mention that travelling is part of ninth house symbolism, even if we travel for any reason other than a quest for ultimate knowledge. When we travel, we are on our way towards the unknown.

Seeking knowledge and wisdom, we will find beliefs and philosophies. Cultures. Sciences. Foreign countries and traditions. Strange ceremonies and magic beverages.

Other worldviews and customs will challenge the validity of ours.

In the third house, learning was comparatively easy. We could know the exact number of bones in a human skeleton (two hundred and six for an adult, about two hundred and seventy at birth, but later some fuse together). Two plus two will always be four. In German a cat is a *Katze,* in Spanish a *gato,* and in French a *chat.*

In the ninth house, things are not so clear. We need explanations. Who are we? What's the meaning of life? Did we just appear, out of the blue, with no other purpose than feeling a bit of pleasure and a lot of pain before disappearing back into the void? Is there a God? Do we have free will? Are we guilty? Should we be ashamed? And if so, why?

What is reality? What are the laws behind the facts? What can we know?

Science provides a number of answers which invariably lead to more questions. Our worldview is never a certainty. It is made up of limited knowledge and a lot of beliefs.

When I was studying psychology, I came across an article entitled 'Implicit theories of personality'. Let me relate the idea. Some people give money to charities. We will likely say that they are *generous.* We think that generosity is a personality trait. However, according to the social scientist personality traits do not exist.

Someone who behaves with generosity in certain circumstances may not behave generously in other circumstances. Someone can be generous with money but mean with their time. Someone can be generous with the members of their family and not with the local community, or vice versa.

If generosity was a personality trait, like we spontaneously assume when we say that someone IS generous, then this trait should be expressed consistently.

Our perception that personalities are made of characteristic traits is only a gross approximation, if not a complete illusion.

In any case, this chapter is not about personality theories, but about the ninth house and the problem of knowledge. Every one of us needs to get an idea of what kind of world we are living in and what kind of beings we are, and it's complicated! We mix knowledge and beliefs, opinions and dogmas to create a map of reality – our worldview – and we navigate through life according to its indications.

A big problem is that we don't have a single and coherent worldview. Instead, we have many fragments.

In one fragment we may believe that God or the Universe will provide for whatever we need. It's written in the Gospel: 'Look for the things of the Heavenly Kingdom and the rest will be added unto you'. If you belong to the Christian faith, these are the words of God and He was not joking.

People belonging to the New Age community say a similar thing, with other words: 'The Universe will provide'...

However, in another fragment of the worldview, it is said that you must work hard to get what you want. You may worship the Word of God on Sundays, you hear how you will be provided for, yet you go to work on Monday anyway.

A further fragment might propose that the Universe won't provide unless you take the trouble to focus your thoughts in order to attract whatever you desire. The law of attraction seems to me nothing but an alternative way of working hard at making things happen.

But what if our current reality is already the manifestation of the best possible compromise between all the contradictory things we want? (That's my personal belief!)

...And in a further fragment of our worldview you can believe that sexual desire is bad, and that the more you desire it the further away from real love you are. (Especially if outer beauty feels more attractive than inner beauty, what a shame!)

In yet another fragment, sexuality is a sacred thing, and all the illustrations accompanying this wonderful statement show only young and beautiful couples about to conflate worship and copulation.

In one fragment, wisdom says that desires must be contained, otherwise they grow without limits and we become their slaves. And in another, that our desires are expressions of our true nature and we should honour them.

One thing is certain: if our worldview is not unified and coherent, there must be holes in it.

More often than not, we use the fragment we prefer according to changing circumstances, and we are not even aware that we have close to no control over the course of our lives.

However, those who keep banging into walls may end up taking a sharp look at their inner Guidance System and realise that the mixture of fragmented knowledge and illusions they have about reality make them nothing but fools.

The quest for truth often starts from there...

22

Tenth House formalities

"*So, Mr. Pierson, what do you do?*"

If someone asks me this question in a social gathering as a way to start a conversation, they are actually asking: *"So, Mr. Pierson, tell me about your MC!"*

According to my answer, they will decide whether it's worth talking more or look for someone else to engage with, and this will have nothing to do with the goodness of my heart or how clever I might be. It's just a question of social status.

In the house system I use, Placidus, the MC is the cusp of the 10th house, and the meaning is the same. As an angle, the MC is more powerful than the rest of the 10th house

Traditionally, the 10th house is the house of career, status and reputation. Moreover it may often represent the mother, which is a bit baffling for the house naturally associated with Saturn, unless you think that the mother is not only the one who nurtures and cares, but also the one who shapes her child's behaviour through demands and interdictions.

In fact it is the shaping function that is represented by the tenth house.

The way we are shaped determines our social status.

We learn our place in society in the first society we are a member of: our family. Unless we work hard later at changing the one thousand habits we learned as malleable children, we become the kind of citizen which corresponds to the kind of member we were in the family-society. (Nothing is more similar to something than its exact opposite, so if that's your case, there is no contradiction.)

Magical Doors

The MC is how we appear from a distance. When I was young, growing up in a small town, everyone knew Doctor Stock. He was the most trusted and the busiest Doctor. He was serious, friendly and competent. Who knew about his moods, tastes, worries, hopes, hobbies? Who knew about his beliefs, his philosophy, his emotions? Most people knew only his MC. He was THE Doctor. He was well loved. He fulfilled his function.

The social roles we play relate to more than the jobs we do; they can be about anything we are known for. Being a committed activist, the best football player on the local team, the winner of a thousand beauty pageants, the one who is always seen feeding the pigeons and talks to nobody...

If a movie director needs extras, they will be defined in MC terms:

'Send me three soldiers, a rapper, two cyclists and a beggar!'

If the three soldiers who first appeared in the background are now interacting with a beautiful girl, the Ascendants appear. One of the soldiers might be cheeky, another might play the wingman and the third might wait and see. The girl might be flirtatious or reserved, friendly or haughty... We now see less of the MCs and more of the ACs.

In sociology, role theory considers that most everyday activities are actually nothing but acting out roles (mother, teacher, waiter, CEO...) Once the role is known, the behaviour can easily be predicted.

Whether or not we fit into the mould is an MC problem. If we don't, we fall into another category. We can be a rebel, an artist, a fool, have special needs... I keep using labels. Saturn is the natural ruler of this house associated with Capricorn. It's all shapes and structures.

You may have to tie a knot around your neck every morning. Maybe you have to wear ugly black shoes that hurt your feet. I never wear a suit and tie, but then I'm a Pisces MC. I hate tight shoes and ties. They are lies to me.

Our role, our social status can be subtle as well. In a group of humans, we can be a leader or a follower, an eccentric, a neither-dominant-nor-submissive individual, or an outcast, a scapegoat...

Similar roles exist in the animal kingdom as well; as a deer or a wolf you can be an alpha male or female, or have a beta status, but you see, I'm still talking in terms of social labels and categories.

To know more about all that, it's time to take sociology classes where group dynamics and role theories should be the most relevant subjects.

23

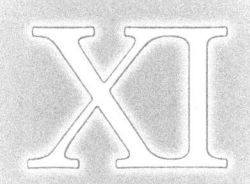

Flavour of the Eleventh House

Imagine... you have four bags full of treats. In the first bag, about 75% of the treats are red, so naturally, you call this bag the Red Bag. Sometimes you pick a yellow, a blue or a green treat from the Red Bag, and it feels weird but never mind, you love your treats so much, you devour them as quickly as a dog.

Same thing with the other bags: the yellow, the blue and the green ones all contain a majority of treats of the right colour plus a few others. Never mind, you love them, you devour them at the speed of light.

Now, as it happens, you've embarked on a spiritual journey. You practise mindfulness. You get into the habit of munching your treats. As your spiritual awareness deepens you become increasingly aware of the tastes.

One day you have an epiphany: all the treats in the red bag are salty. All the treats in the yellow bag are slightly acidic. All the treats in the green bag are a little bitter and all the treats from the blue bag are sugary. They are all delicious in their own way.

Now you know what every single treat belonging to a particular bag has in common with all the others. You can make predictions with a hundred per cent success rate.

Of course, you are not a dog. Neither am I, but sometimes our minds are like hungry dogs. We gobble up information without munching and we forget to taste the flavour of reality.

Our bags of treats are not four but twelve, they are the houses of the horoscope. We know by heart lists of colourful key words but we're never quite sure which ones will apply.

This little metaphor is itself a treat – it was one for me when it popped up in my head. I hope it was one for you as well!

It is a bitter sweet treat actually. By this I mean it may well be found in two bags. I started to write it as an introduction to the eleventh house, and here I am thinking that it actually belongs in the ninth, Jupiter's house.

With Jupiter, we're working on our worldview. We're seeking the truth. What are these bags really about?

Jupiter is the grandson of Uranus. They have features in common. The eleventh house, naturally ruled by Grandpa, is an Air house. Air symbolises the mental plane, along with the social dimension of life. Houses can overlap.

When a Truth Seeker finds the Truth, they stop being a Truth Seeker. When he or she becomes enlightened… it's not Sagittarius anymore, it's Aquarius. Insight! Breakthrough! Eureka! Vision! Eleventh house!

Anyway. Let's breathe for a few seconds.

………

….

….

…Let's now pick a few treats from the 11th house…

Traditionally, the eleventh is the House of Friends. Some friendships are love stories without the sex part, and without the kind of tight commitment which involves having to call and warn that you are going to come home a bit later than usual when it's the case (and it shouldn't be the case too often).

With friends, you can let time pass by without giving news, reappear when you do and all is fine. You're free. You're welcome. You can breathe.

Friendship is simple. You talk about love. Love is complicated. Talking about it with a friend is simple. You talk about all your hopes and wishes (*Hopes and wishes* is another traditional meaning of the eleventh house).

Flavour of the Eleventh House

The most complex kinds of hopes and wishes are called *Ideologies*. They always involve the vision of a bright future for a humanity freed of its chains.

Ideologies may be born from the realization that personal hopes and wishes, which are always about thriving, living free and love, can't happen in just any context. Society must be a favourable environment... Therefore, revolution is needed! (It's good to put the world to rights with friends).

'Never doubt that a small group of thoughtful, committed citizens can change the world; indeed, it's the only thing that ever has.'

Margaret Mead, cultural anthropologist, Sun conjunct Uranus and Mercury in Sagittarius and the eleventh house, Moon and Venus in Aquarius.

The eleventh is also the house of groups.

A group can be a choir, a football club, a political party, a charity, a public speaking club, a gathering of witches, a gang, a cooperative, a language exchange club, a congregation, the scientific community... (the largest groups are called society and the human species).

You can sing in a choir without being personally involved with everyone. New people join, others leave. After a few years, it's still the same choir, but mostly different people. You're just a cell in an organism. We are individual units belonging to something greater: a choir, a party, a culture, a species, a universe...

Molecules of water are magnets. They stick to each other. Molecules in crystals (Earth element) are solidly bonded together, they can't move at all. With the Air element, there is so much space.

If you miss closeness, remember: with more distance, there is less pressure. You can be whoever you want to be.

If you start focusing your energy on actually making a dream come true, if you get romantically involved with someone in particular, if you leave the realm of infinite freedom and potentials to make something happen, you leave the eleventh house. The fifth house is just across the road.

Similarly, at the level of the mind, you won't remain attached to old thinking habits. Your mother will keep calling the red bag 'Red bag' and the yellow bag 'Yellow bag' until her final breath. – but not you, eleventh house dweller!

In your head, ideas are like friends: they don't always have to be tied up together. Codes, customs, traditions, habits, conventions don't have to apply all the time. A thinking pattern is somehow built with mental Lego bricks. Most people don't dare break them and make new ones. In the eleventh you're at the right place to do just that.

When I was a boy, one day I dipped grapes in mustard. I liked grapes and I liked mustard so I wondered whether I would like grapes with mustard. I was immediately told to stop by a stepmother who couldn't bear the idea of not doing things the way they should be done.

Vade Retro Saturnas! I want to experiment with the taste of grapes with mustard!

It's always possible to break down mental elements and recombine them. That's what thinkers and inventors do. Nothing is heavy in here. You don't need bulldozers to change a plan. You can put wings on horses and caterpillars on unicorns. You might think that maybe the earth is round when everyone swears it's flat. You can design new technologies.

The mental plane, the immensity of the sky, friends, groups, hopes and wishes, ideologies, utopias, progress, individuality, communities, the universe within and without... Flavours of the eleventh house...

XII

24

Our connection with the Great Mystery: the Twelfth House

The twelfth house is a most dreaded house, even more so than the eighth. I wonder why.

In the zodiac, Scorpio's reputation is worse than Pisces though, so why is the reverse true when it comes to the analogous houses?

By the way, being analogous is not at all the same as equating. The signs are universal energies or principles. We can see them at work everywhere, in humans, in nature, in life.

The houses have more concrete meanings. These meanings have something of the spirit of the sign they are analogous to. Taurus is a sign that wants substance. This can apply to many things. The second house is traditionally about earning money. This is adding substance in practice. We live in societies where money has value. In a tribe of hunters and gatherers, the second house would be about hunting and gathering.

The twelfth house is a Watery house.

The Water element talks about deep feelings and emotions, longings, cravings, instincts, deeply ingrained memories from childhood, from our ancestors or from past lives along with connections with dimensions of the universal soul we wouldn't even suspect existed...

Beyond words, the twelfth is a world of music and images.

Let's choose a thread to follow, knowing it's not the only one. Quite often, with water, there is a surface, there is above the surface, and there is below. Expect to be confused...

We often repeat *'As above, so below'* thinking *'above'* means up in the heavens and *'below'* down here. However, *'above'* can also be right here, the world where we can breathe and see, and *'below'* can be the invisible and mysterious world of deep down.

The world is reflected upside down when the surface of the water is still and smooth like a mirror, so maybe we could also put the old saying upside down: *'As below, so above'*. *'Below'* is below the surface of appearances. What is cause and what is effect is a chicken or egg problem, our side is the chicken side, *'below'*, or within, is the egg side.

The dramas, the conflicts, the attractions and loathings, the falls in and out of love, the alliances and betrayals, the shapes and abilities of our bodies, the endless repetition of routines, the walls and the checkpoints, the abuses and the bureaucracies... All life as we know it may be nothing but the chicken of our eggs, kept and nurtured by Water, hatching and growing according to the rhythm of the stars. Some eggs may have been waiting for many lives.

In the twelfth house is our connection with the deepest Mystery.

What is deepest is also highest. Heraclitus, the Greek philosopher, once said: *'The way up and the way down are one and the same'*. I take this as meaning that whether you take your spiritual journey as a journey of exploration of what is deep, or as the climbing of a sacred mountain on top of which the Great Spirit of the Heavens is waiting for you, one way or another, you're doing the same thing. When you don't know where is up and where is down, when you can't know within from without, you become so lost you can only pray and ask for guidance. We need to feel confused to let go of our helpless ego and let a bigger hand take ours. *'Unless you change and become like little children, you will never enter the kingdom of heaven'* said Jesus.

Life comes from Water and Water is always pregnant. Some dreams may be called karmic, we gave them to Water once upon a time... What we do to others leaves us with a lingering dream, the dream that the same thing may happen to us. Maybe it won't happen. Maybe we'll tackle the issue directly in the world of dreams, (if we are able to see what is in gestation

Our connection with the Great Mystery: the Twelfth House

there), and choose what we keep nurturing and what we better defuse or transform. What is in store in the universal womb? One way or another, we have to face what's roaming the waters. In meditation, before it grows too real, is the best option.

Not everything is karmic as far as I understand. We are doing more than just dealing with the past. We also have dreams which are simply our dreams, our potentials.

We can't see what's below the surface. We can go fishing with the Fisher King, for healing, because spiritual seeking starts with suffering – the wakeup call. We can't see below the surface but we can imagine, as humans do when confronted with the unknown, all kinds of things, treasures, remedies, monsters, mermaids, genies trapped in bottles... These images, which happen to be the language spoken by our so-called *'unconscious mind'*, exist without words, without clear consciousness, without us being able to take some distance to look at them. We are immersed in the dream world all the time. The world of our most intimate subjectivity is so familiar that we don't even notice it's there and for us it's deep down in the dark. How could a fish notice there is water? It would have to pop its head above the surface, and see the difference. Sometimes a fish does just that and speaks to a puzzled fisherman to tell him secrets powerful enough to change his whole life. Let's hope the fisherman is wise...

The symbol for the fourth house and Cancer is the crab. This animal is seen out of the water when the tide is low. It appears and runs on firm ground. The origins remain mysterious but at least we see what we get. A baby came out of the water, took its first breath and now it's crawling on its hands and knees, a little crab carrying with him an ocean of ancestral memories. The symbol for the twelfth and Pisces is two fish swimming in opposite directions. As we appeared out of the ocean, so we will return to the world of no limits and no differences.

Death, however, is usually associated with the eighth house and Scorpio. In the eighth, however, we still speak of the other world, from which we are separated by a veil which, they say, is at its thinnest at Samhain or Halloween. On the other side of the veil are spirits with which mediums communicate. You can get news from your loved ones after they have passed away. In the eighth, death means transformation. According to those more knowledgeable than me, after we die, we go to the astral plane, and there we may still have a sense of being ourselves. We will catch up with our ancestors and sort out the conditions of our next incarnation.

The twelfth house seems to mean something even deeper, something similar to what Buddhists mean when they say that the very notion of self is an illusion, as everyone of us is nothing but the whole universe manifesting. We are just a wave on the surface of the ocean, but nothing is permanent, this wave too will pass. When we know we are the ocean, we are fine. When we don't, we fear annihilation... That's why we may fear the twelfth more than the eighth.

Planets in the twelfth may make us feel lost, unable to find expression, disoriented, but they may also help us express ourselves through art, music or poetry, which we can't practise without being inspired.

The twelfth is a world of music and images.

Service to others – and especially those in need – is another positive way to express twelfth house placements.

There is a logic behind being lost, needing to be saved and saving. Now, even saving may be just another illusion...

Healing or anything we label *'spiritual'* works very well as a twelfth house expression. Placements in the twelfth may indicate the great trials and suffering which make us search for healing and/or become healers, priests, bridges, channels.

Placements in the twelfth may evoke little cells, because, as in monasteries, those who dedicate their lives to contemplate this ocean of Mystery need to be contained in little cells and follow strict rules. There is a law of balance that needs to be respected, the fish swim simultaneously in both directions.

When the cell is not in a monastery, it may be in a prison or a psychiatric hospital. Nothing is closer to wisdom and spiritual enlightenment than delusion and madness as both the wise and the mad free themselves from the socially accepted norms...

A laboratory or a hidden space may be conveyed by the twelfth house.

Occultists talk about the sphere of illusions that students have to confront. Illusions are another Neptunian meaning that we can find at all levels of expression, from the basic deception of the conman who makes you believe giving them all your money is a good idea, to the hallucinations and delusions associated with mental illness, via extra marital affairs and the artificial paradises of alcohol, drugs, compulsive sex or any addictions.

Now, funnily enough, the twelfth house can also mean that you are working in a hotel or a restaurant. Even if it's a business, hotels and hospitals are places of hospitality.

Neptune sometimes simply means liquids, oils, alcohols (called spirits), perfumes... If your business has a twelfth house flavour, you may be selling essential oils or investing in petroleum companies.

Sometimes, the ocean is also a literal interpretation of Neptune, Pisces or the twelfth house. A twelfth houser may be a sailor. Mars in the twelfth may serve in the Navy, or roam the oceans with Greenpeace. Ask the mermaids.

With Neptune, Pisces, and the twelfth house, we want to return to Paradise – all illusions and escapism may come from the idea that we can take shortcuts. Hence addictions and depressions...

Sacrifice is another big spiritual theme. Sometimes we sacrifice ourselves for others, sometimes we sacrifice something we are attached to in order to be able to attach ourselves to something higher. Sometimes we are just scapegoats, victims, sacrificed by others against our will, but if it's in our chart...

But maybe, to get a feel of the twelfth we should stop using this Mercurial mind (which should now be happy enough with this list) and go listen to some music. Choose the most compelling music, the one you love most, and get carried away. Soon you will be so entranced that you will have forgotten that you have a body, a name, a yesterday and a tomorrow. No *must*, no *should*, no *guilt*, no *shame*, no *have to* remain in consciousness.

Only oneness, only communion.

We are waves...

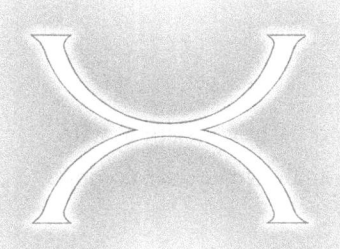

25
Analogy rather than equivalence

When I started to learn astrology, I accepted the notion sometimes known as the *'astrological alphabet'* which simply states that there are similarities between signs and houses. The same archetype is at work with, Aries for instance, Mars its ruler, and the first house. Mars then can be called the *'natural ruler'* of the first house.

In *Saturn: A New Look at an Old Devil* Liz Greene gives similar interpretations of Saturn's placements in signs and houses.

This view has been attacked as a modern invention having nothing to do with traditional knowledge, a lazy approach and a few other choice words. However, the main argument of people dismissing the astrological alphabet is that houses and signs are not equivalent. This is a fundamental misunderstanding. Equivalence means identity, not similarity. If you say that *'the camel is the ship of the desert'* it is a metaphor. There is a similarity between a camel in the desert and a ship on the ocean. It is a lazy attack to simply state that camels are not ships in order to dismiss the validity of the metaphor. Of course, camels have no sails and ships no legs. Still, they are doing something similar. They carry people and merchandises over long distances.

The astrological alphabet is extremely useful. If camels and ships were astrological symbols, you would know, upon seeing them both appear in a particular chart, that carrying goods and people over long distances is an especially important theme. What is important is repeated. If you come across a chart with Mercury dominant and important placements in both Virgo and the sixth house, you know you are onto something with sixth house themes.

It seems to me that this way of reasoning is actually consistent with traditional esoteric thinking. The same argument against the astrological alphabet could apply to secondary progressions.

Secondary progressions are based on the analogy between two fundamental cycles in our lives: days and years. Days are not equivalent to years! In this predictive technique, the position of planets a certain number of days after our birth becomes the position of those progressed planets for the same number of years after we were born. How we lived our thirty-fifth day, for example, is a prediction about how our thirty-fifth year will unfold.

The law of analogy is an old principle of hermetic philosophy. It's often expressed as: *'As above, so below, as within, so without'*.

It can also be: *'As in the cosmos, so in the microcosm'* which is why astrologers see a correlation between a certain individual's traits and the placement of planets in the heavens at the moment of their birth.

Correspondences do not mean causes and effects. Transiting Saturn does not cause delays in our lives any more than delays cause the transit of Saturn.

If you're using a method of divination like the Yi Jing, the way the sticks fall at the moment you're asking a question reflect the quality of the time – and so does the question itself. Therefore, there is a correspondence between question and how the sticks fall.

You could look at the chart of the moment you are asking your question and this *horary* chart would be another expression of the quality of the moment.

The law of correspondences can also be expressed as: *'As in the small cycles, so in the big ones'*. When the small cycle is the day and the big one the year, there is a correspondence. It's obvious if you think that spring is like morning, summer like midday, autumn like evening and winter like night. We do think and feel like this. The law of analogy implies that the way we think and feel about the world is not random nonsense but meaningful reality.

Analogy rather than equivalence

In our natal charts, the daily cycle is shown by the position of the houses. Someone born when the Sun is about to reach the peak of its daily trajectory has the Sun in the tenth house. Someone born when the Sun is about to set has it in the seventh house, and if the Sun was about to rise, it is in the first house.

The houses divide the day into twelve sections, and the signs of the zodiac divide the year. There must be correspondences between houses and signs. The first house is the first to rise in the morning, as is Aries in the 'morning of the year'. The second house will be the second to rise, as Taurus following Aries in spring...

Now, zodiacal signs are symbols. What they express is also analogical. A Sun in Capricorn says that the individual central power is *like* a sea goat, which evokes the idea to start from the bottom and climb high. There is room for interpretation!

Similarly, the Sun in the tenth house is reaching as high as it can. There is analogy. Again, this does not mean equivalence. Houses are day to day life, they are the 'boots on the ground' of the energies, their most concrete expression. Signs are seasons of the energies; they are more indicative of an atmosphere or mind-set.

Houses answer the question *'What is happening here?'* and signs provide the answer to *'How is this happening?'*

The distinction is real, but not absolute. Sometimes, how we do things has a real impact on what we are actually doing, and what we are doing certainly influences how to proceed...

In the following chapters we will be musing on the signs of the zodiac...

26

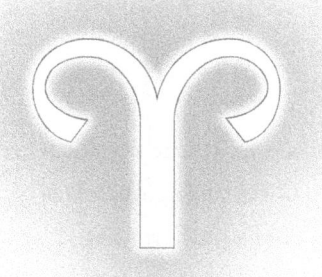

Aries

Once upon a time, Aries!

Before the beginning, there is no time.

Without time nothing can start.

The absolute absoluteness of the eternal present moment is, and this is it.

At some point, however, there must be a starting point. God says *"Let there be light!"*, the Tao splits into Yang and Yin, a Primordial Ancestor slaughters a Primordial Dragon from the remains of which plants will grow. One way or another something happens. That's the Aries moment. The first one.

Once upon a time, out of the Divine Blue, existence burst out. Here! Something! Movement! Time! Space! Energy! Aries!

As it extracts itself from the eternal totality, Aries proclaims: *"I am me! And the rest... is not me! Differentiation! Action!"*

This beginning will be repeated, echoed, renewed, again and again, as the opposite pull, like a rubber band, holds Aries back and makes its strength necessary.

As Newton elegantly put it: *"For every action, there is an equal and opposite reaction"*.

Once upon a time, an embryo was floating in amniotic liquid; it didn't know what time it was when something big happened: it was pushed firmly and forcefully headfirst into the unknown; it took a first breath and shouted: *"Here I am!"*

The nostalgia for life before birth, a deep memory of a lost paradise, will express itself as *regressive tendencies* in times of difficulty. If we believe

Joseph Campbell, author of *The Hero with a Thousand Faces*, all the mythical dragons we must face and slay on our heroic journey of becoming ourselves are symbols of these regressive tendencies towards being undifferentiated.

When was the last time you did something for the first time?

Nowadays it's possible to spend an entire childhood without seeing a ram. Before, people knew it well. It was the sheep leader, a male with hard horns on its head and a marked tendency to charge.

Wise men of old recognised a signature in the behaviour of this animal. It was an illustration of the cosmic story, a symbol of this fundamental ingredient in life's kitchen: a strong focus of energy, a powerful move forward, an intense affirmation of existence.

Life is a succession of beginnings, big and small. The beginning of a story is followed by the beginning of every sentence followed by the beginning of every word and of every sound and every second. Aries, like all cosmic energies, is always happening here and now...

A sunray is doing Aries as it moves forward, away from the centre. Mars rules Aries. The symbol for Mars shows a circle, a symbol of totality, and an arrow moving away from it, in a particular direction. We are sunrays. We are the Sun and everyone is a ray moving away... Without rays the Sun would be but a legless flea.

Mars is in domicile in Aries. Aries is to Mars what a house – or a room – is to the human who lives in it. The room is a living picture of the soul of the dweller.

Mars also lives in Scorpio: planetary energies have a Yin and a Yang side, apart from the Sun and apart from the Moon which are each other's Yin and Yang. We are not too sure about the transpersonal planets. Let's come back to Aries for now.

All cosmic energies can be seen in the big things and in the little details alike. Hitting a nail on the head is Aries energy, literally and metaphorically.

Aries expresses itself at all levels: physical, emotional, mental and spiritual or creative.

Aries will not systematically mean the naked aggression of the macho male dealing blows to other males for the privilege to powerfully push his sexual energy into females. But when this is the case, Aries means it. Competition, leadership, action.

Emotionally Aries can manifest as desire or anger, as fight or flight instinct.

Thinking is very much an Aries thing. Think of it: thoughts are focused energy. Thinking takes us outside of ourselves. In meditation we strive to come back to our inner centre, the third eye at the centre of the head and the heart at the centre of the chest... but as soon as the monkey mind resumes its chatter, we're running outside of ourselves again!

Take your head in your hands in the position of thinking hard, and feel... Where are you? And where is the centre?

Thinking is useful though, especially when it's not disconnected from the heart. Good thinking leads to decision-making and action...

The symbol of Aries – the ram – and of Mars – the arrow pointing outwards from a point in the circle – are here to talk to us directly. Symbols show us what they are about.

Let's look at life and see! Where is Aries?

27

And then, Taurus

Aries is Fire, pure energy. Aries is Cardinal, pure beginning.

After a volcanic eruption, lava becomes fertile soil.

Aries, fiery impulse for independent existence turns into Taurus as it materialises.

Fire becomes Earth. Spirit wraps itself in bodies. Spirit acquires substance. It takes form and holds a particular shape.

Now you have a body.

A body is not what you are. It is something you identify with because you're wrapped up in it.

A body is a piece of clothing. On one hand it is really you, dear oriental princess or you, dazzling northern light, because it speaks your special brand of elegance and beauty. Your clothes express your spirit, yes, but still, before you can dance in that dress, you must have it.

In Earth and Fixed Taurus, you acquire substance, like a genie, a gust of wind from a bottle transforming into a muscular giant and about to grant wishes... but that's storytelling. After you were born, you had to eat, suck at the breast and put on weight. Your ego had to do the same, psychologically. Acquiring, adding, accumulating, owning substance. Substance is the word.

You are you, baby, because you *have*...

You have lovely little hands, beautiful eyes, one or two dolls, a teddy bear, a Mum and a Dad, a rattle, a soft snake, a crocodile and a special hat; carry on like that and you will have a bank account, a house and a car, a company, a family, people you'll call *"mine"*...

You'll have, therefore you will be and maybe you will measure your worth in money.

(There was a time where your material worth was counted in heads of cattle, bulls being the most valuable ones.)

Keep adding value! Skills, knowledge, qualities, anything you can acquire and add to yourself will make you feel safe about being real.

Like a growing onion you will add layer after layer to your ego. You'll be peeled in Scorpio like Inanna visiting Ereshkigal and become dizzy at the void if you don't remember spirit.

...What if nature was the Great Spirit's body?

Aum...

Nature is Spirit dressed up in trees, rivers, mountains, clouds, plants, animals and us.

Call me animist or pantheist if you want. That's certainly a philosophy that suits Taurus well. God is Life and Life is within.

To sum it up, the energy of Taurus is spirit slowing down and putting on weight.

All energies can go too far. A pure outburst of creative energy slowing down and putting on weight can make you appear as Aphrodite, sensual and beautiful like the Goddess of love with attractive curves in all the right places.

Keep slowing down, put on a bit more weight and you may get Ella Fitzgerald. If you're so young her name doesn't ring a bell, she had a wonderful voice. She was rather plump, she had four planets in Taurus and she was a true jazz miracle.

Beyond Ella, Spirit would be better off stopping slowing down and piling on the pounds, unless Spirit's plan is to end up in the Guinness Book of Records as world champion of the Couch Potato Race. Switch quickly to Gemini energy before it's too late!

Taurus rules the throat. You eat and then you sing. Pleasure goes both ways.

Venus rules Taurus. The symbol is a circle representing totality, or spirit, and a cross, representing matter, underneath the circle.

Female sexuality is like a potent magnetic field, drawing sexual energy towards it symbolically, into the mouth or the vagina. I don't believe, like Freud did, that sexual motivations are everywhere, but that sexual basic facts are very clear (and crude) manifestations of the archetypal pattern: here, it's about taking in. It can be a penis, semen, food, a new idea, a delivery brought to the door of the house or new members being welcomed by a club, the energy is "taking in."

It is also a binding energy.

Traditional gender roles, to which exceptions apply (exceptions can't exist without rules), illustrate archetypal energies very well. They give to the male the *"chasing"* role... but instead of being an innocent prey, in this game, the female is a trapper. Aries wants to be independent and Taurus wants attachment.

Earthy rhythm, earthy customs...

28

One, two, three... Gemini!

The Twins open great eyes.

In the beginning, Aries, intense focus of energy moving forward was like a sunbeam, moving away from the centre, do you remember?

What would the Sun look like if it had only one ray? There are many!

Taurus slowed down Aries and made it dense, physical, material...

Now the twins are waking up, brand new to the world and very curious. They exclaim in surprise: "We are many!"

Yes, we are many, as numerous sunbeams shooting away from the Sun.

Two is the first step away from one. Two is the beginning – and the symbol – of *many*.

In its infinite wisdom, the Great Spirit made twins. The zodiac is a picture book for children. Each picture shows something essential. Twins make us wonder:

Are we the same? Are we other?

The answer is: We're both!

We are all the same. We are all different. We are one. We are many.

From now on, Gemini will be busy connecting.

The simplest formulation for Gemini energy is:

There is one, there is another, and now we are connecting these two.

This applies to anything, from atoms to stars.

There is a city, there is another city, there is a road between the two. Gemini rules roads, ways, little journeys...

There are people, there are tools, people have hands, tools have handles. Gemini rules hands, arms and shoulders.

There are events, there are people and to connect them there are journalists and newspapers, local gossip, Chinese whispers...

Gemini's glyph looks like the numeral for two, however Gemini comes third in the zodiac: two, plus the relationship between them, makes three.

Gemini energy is especially important for humans. We talk.

We name. Naming was Adam's job in paradise, before the unfortunate affair with the apple.

There is a thing, for example an animal that goes *"meow"*, there is a sound: [kaet] Gemini connects the two: this connection is called *"meaning"*.

The thing can be an object, a plant, an animal, a human, an action, an emotion, a quality... All we can see, hear, touch, taste, smell or feel gets a sign equivalent in another world we call *"mind"*.

In this other world we keep interacting, so to speak, in the Air. We exchange signs.

I can say *"cat"* and this simple sound will have an impact on your mind: an image looking more or less like a cat will appear in your consciousness. You'll see what I mean and smile. I can go on and make you see all kinds of things and feel all kinds of feelings, just with words. What a great power!

I love you.

Just by speaking we can heal, hurt, suggest, motivate, entertain, inspire... Words are energy pipes.

Gemini is a mutable sign. As Stephen Arroyo explains so well, Cardinal signs generate energy, Fixed signs concentrate energy and Mutable signs distribute energy.

We spend most of our lives in the air. In the mind. In social interaction. It's vast like infinite space and we don't know the way out. We're constantly juggling.

We can go too far. The cat in your mind may look less and less like a real cat. You may not even take the trouble to see a cat. (Are you seeing one now?)

Blah blah blah. We can keep on and live in a web of signs connected with other signs, and the latter connected with even more signs, to the extent that the whole network may as well be completely disconnected from any tangible reality. This is called *"schizophrenia"*.

Aries, energy. Taurus, substance. Gemini, information. With these three we've all we need to create worlds.

Taurus was concerned with accumulating substance. There is now what I have and there is what you have; we can trade!

I'm not going to let you know how much I desire what you have, I'm going to pretend that I don't value your stuff as much as you value mine (I can see it in your eyes). I'll make you happy and myself even more so... What sport!

Hermes-Mercury is the God of merchants, and also of liars and thieves, to name but a few. This trickster is the wittiest of the Gods!

Translators always know two versions of the same story.

What if I divided the world into two categories? On one side, Me. On the other side, The Environment. Between them, the first and most vital connection is the breath.

Breathing exercises are good to calm down the nervous system and the mind. It's all ruled by Gemini. Becoming silent is the way out of the mind.

Consciousness is born with this third sign.

The word *"conscious"* comes from the Latin *"conscius"*, made of *"con"* meaning *"with"* and *"scio"* meaning *"to know"*.

To be conscious is to know with. Consciousness is always consciousness of something.

Is consciousness of nothing still consciousness? Or just Sciousness? God knows!

Esoteric teachings say that the conscious mind lies between the unconscious and the superconscious. Once more we're in between.

Some people say "God is within ourselves. We are God."

I agree... and I don't. The metaphysical and zodiacal story I have set out to tell states that life surges from the eternal and absolute Mystery and becomes individualized, so yes, that's how I see it: God becomes Life and Life becomes us, yes yes yes.

However, this little consciousness who says *"I am me"* is far from knowing everything. If I had to create a functioning nervous system out of a heap of atoms, I would be rather embarrassed.

So how come there is a working nervous system right here? If I am God and I didn't do it, who did it? Yes, there must be a superconscious dimension. A parent. We are brothers and sisters. We are learning. Life is a school. Gemini rules over learning and schools...

We are God's fingertips.

By the way, if you think your brain is just the result of a series of random mutations you are an infinite monkey. As Einstein put it: *"God does not play dice."*

I am, you are, we are little consciousnesses awakening. We are babies. We are twins. We are many. The Great Spirit is One. We are the other side of the Great Coin. There is a link between the two. We are same and others.

Do you feel a bit scattered? Don't worry...

29

Cancer: All life starts in water...

With Cancer, things start to become a bit crazy.

Cancer is the fourth sign.

It's also the second first sign: Cancer is cardinal, which means it's a Once-upon-a-time-the-story-starts-with-me sign.

We'll observe four Cardinal-Fixed-Mutable stories as we go around the zodiacal wheel.

Once upon a time, Cancer! Life starts in Water.

By the way, we are talking a language of symbols here. It's not modern science and doesn't have to be.

Modern science is good with everything that can be objectively measured, and not relevant to psychic or spiritual realities. For instance, it has not been able to explain consciousness. Every so often someone claims that science has demonstrated that consciousness was produced by the brain. It's not true. This has not been proven at all.

When you destroy the brain, consciousness disappears; when you destroy a radio, the program can't be heard anymore, however you can't kill the entire BBC staff by hitting your radio with a hammer.

Something is sure: take for example the colour blue. When we look at the sky on a clear day, blue exists as a sensation in our consciousness. However, nothing is blue in the brain. There may be neurological circuits meaning "blue", like a code... but it's all grey in there.

Where does this blue exist, if it is in our consciousness and not in our brain? Science can't touch that. But it's there.

Modern science has its limits. What is the equation for the quantity of artistic creativity you get when you sublimate three kilograms of raw sexual desire? How many litres of motherly love does it take to get a baby to sleep?

Science can't offer answers, but we can feel inner realities. We know dreams and speak the language of symbols, images, fantasies... which are reflections of the subjective world which is the world we really live in, made of what we feel within.

What we feel and what we felt within. What was once a present moment is still there, imprinted as memory. Our own personal story lives within. Under the conscious, the subconscious...

Cancer is *Yin*. Occidental tradition says *feminine*, which evokes *taking from outside in, nurturing inside and giving birth.*

Once upon an eternal time, all life started in water.

Aries started as a spiritual sunbeam bursting out from the sun-heart of the Great Spirit. Cancer starts from deep within material reality, in the womb of the Great Mother.

The zodiac is a wheel, Aries may start it, but it does so nine months after Cancer.

Once upon a time, fecundation. Then gestation...

Then giving birth (or being born). Then nurturing (or being nurtured)...

Then getting old and being cared for in turn (or growing up and becoming a parent in turn)

Then dying and becoming an ancestor (or burying and honouring the lineage) ...

Then being born again, wave after wave, generation after generation...

In only one word this cyclical energy is called *"Reproduction"*.

It is somehow the opposite of *"Creation"*, the energy of Fire. It's squaring it, actually.

Look at the crab. It has claws and a hard shell. The flesh is tender within. It walks sideways. There are good meanings to be derived from these observations, but what are we doing breaking the crab down into its constituents? Analytical thinking is not the way.

Let's think the other way round and take a step or two backwards... Jupiter is exalted in Cancer, so let's look at the bigger picture from a distance.

The crab is on the shore. The tide is low. When the tide was high, we couldn't see it. When the tide returns, the crab will disappear again. It lives with the ebb and flow, sometimes immersed, sometimes running sideways... What's wrong with changing moods? It's just sea life.

The Moon is shining above, sometimes waxing, sometimes waning, attracting the waters and then letting them go... The Moon rules in Cancer.

Who wouldn't think of women and their monthly cycles?

All life starts in Water. All life starts in a womb, or in an egg. In a safe space, a cocoon. The purpose is not to stay in there forever but still, small is beautiful, cubs and babies are vulnerable and mothers incredibly sensitive to their needs. Or should be.

Remember *cocoon, vulnerable* and *sensitive* as key words.

All energies can go too far and going too far with Cancer is not going anywhere, just staying put, small and vulnerable, needy with Mummy.

Escaping in imagination into the world of Peter Pan.

Or devouring, smothering, overprotecting, castrating, clinging to the beginning of the cycle, digging heels in against the course of time... My baby will always be my baby!

Nostalgia...

Memory also reproduces. We can conjure up emotionally charged images and relive the past.

Another kind of memory reproduces patterns, for the better or the cursed...

Imagination was born from memory. If you can remember a horse, if you can remember a horn, if you can remember gluing, then you can imagine a unicorn.

Astrology is a language of symbols, like dreams, myths, religious narratives and fairy tales.

Magical Doors

In a world of fantasies, the real contents of the psyche are dancing like fairies or witches around a fire under the Full Moon in the forest.

Fairy tales and mythologies are real because our fears and desires, our hopes, cravings and blisses, our aspirations and temptations, everything we can feel, from the greatest suffering to the eternity of ecstasy is reproduced and represented through stories which unfold according to very old laws... With Cancer we remember and tell the stories.

One day my prince will come, one day Jesus will be back, one day at the end of the long night the light will be born again, the lion and the lamb will lie down together, my baby, my sweet little baby, one day I'll be old, one day we will die, for now hold me tight, for now never let me go...

Life starts and ends in Water.

It's symbolic language. It's a mistake to look for exact and constant interpretations of planets in signs. You may just as easily try to make ropes of water and tie your boat to a post of smoke! Symbols are magical doors. They won't always open on the same scenery. There is a subtle thread from one interpretation to another. The best we can do is try to get the spirit, with the Great Spirit's help. Understanding is a spiritual path.

30

Leo: Life is a spiritual show

All the world's a stage, and all the men and women merely players: they have their exits and their entrances; and one man in his time plays many parts...

— William Shakespeare

Life is indeed a theatre.

It's not only humans who perform on that stage. The smallest blade of grass makes its entrance when it appears on the surface of the earth after the rain.

Esoteric teachings say that humans have many bodies. The physical body is the densest of all. Like plants we have an etheric body. More subtle is the astral or emotional body, then we have the mental body and so on.

The comedian is more than the costume. Who are we? What is Self? Beyond bodies, what is pure spirit?

Let me ask you this again, in another way. Leo is ruled by the Sun. The symbol for the Sun is a circle with a dot at the centre. If you wander in London, you often come across boards with maps of the vicinity; on every map, there is a dot within a circle, with the words:

"You are here."

"Here" is where the dot is. The circle makes the dot conspicuous.

An astrology chart is a map. The dot within the circle likewise indicates: *"You are here"*. You, your authentic Self is the heart of the Sun.

Take a magnifying glass and look at this dot. Once bigger, it doesn't look like a dot anymore. It's a round shape. Its periphery is a circle. Dip the tip of a needle in ink and make a dot at the centre of the dot. Your dot has become a circle with a dot at the centre.

Please repeat the operation a multitude of times in your mind.

OK? Now, try to hold the idea of the perfect dot in your mind. This dot is the absolute centre. Look at it with a cosmic microscope. Your dot is infinitely small, its diameter is zero. Therefore, it doesn't exist. However, you are there. You are Spirit. You are essence and with the circle, you come into existence. To exist (from Latin *ex-* and *-iste*) means to be out. To be means to be.

Trying to evoke mental images of dots that have no thickness at all or of a spirit without substance wrapped up in layers of subtle envelopes are ways to get our ordinary mind puzzled and to stimulate our intuition: Spirit is there, just beyond our grasp. It is the dot at the centre of the mandala. (In Sanskrit, the word for "circle" is "mandala".)

Now that we have done our best, like dedicated salmon, to swim upstream to try and intuit Source, we can let ourselves go with the downstream flow from Source to Matter, from dot to circle.

If you have calm waters nearby, it's a good time to throw a pebble and look at the series of circles expanding around the point of impact. You can chant OM as you do.

Creation story:

Let there be light!

Let there be warmth! Let there be shapes and colours! Let there be bodies, souls and puzzled minds! Let there be Leo! Roar! Here we are!

Out of nothing, intense creative fire is shooting rays in all directions…

Let there be earth, plants and animals!

And let there be, created in the image of God, creative creatures!

Let there be singers, dancers, musicians, composers, painters, artists! Let there be kings and queens of creation!

The material world is a mirror in which Spirit contemplates itself.

Or it's just Brahma having fun manifesting…

Leo: Life is a spiritual show

The world is a stage.

Sunrays are bursting out in all directions, each of them focused in its own particular way and by doing so, expresses itself as Mars-Aries.

Each sunbeam then takes on substance, wraps itself in bodies from the more subtle level to dense physical reality and that's the energy of Venus and Taurus.

Once incarnated sunrays become aware of the space between them and of the multiplicity of their expressions. In Gemini, connections are made in the outside world whilst an inner space appears: the mind.

In Cancer, second cardinal sign of beginnings, we see the three previous stages happening in the realm of the Moon: she is the matrix, the maternal, material environment, the womb in which the solar creative impulse focuses, taking substance and form.

The Moon is the Sun's feminine side, the Sun is the Moon's masculine side. In the zodiac, the other traditional planets all rule over two signs, one of masculine polarity (Fire or Air) and the other of feminine polarity (Earth or Water). Only the Sun and the Moon rule over only one single sign each, and belong unequivocally to only one of the two cosmic polarities: masculine and feminine, or Yin and Yang. They are one.

So, we could say that the Sun is the dot within the circle, and that the Moon is the circle around the dot. A cycle is a circle unfolding in time. The Moon is the archetype of all cycles.

The Sun creates through the Moon and the Moon gives birth to the Sun. Unto us a child is born...

However, what the Sun creates today will be good but for a certain amount of time only. Then, hardened and stiffened by Saturn's law, the creation of yesterday may interfere with the Sun's creation of tomorrow.

The Moon repeats the past. Therapies consist of dealing with patterns we produce and reproduce again and again even though they no longer serve us.

Dane Rudhyar tells us that at the New Moon the Moon receives a new Solar impulse to give it form and substance. Then, the first crescent phase is a phase of fighting the ghosts of the past.

The Spiritual King, call it Lord, or Self, or Divine Spark within, or Conscious Creator, stands at the centre. From the heart, everything starts. To the heart we need to return each time we get carried away a little bit too far by the centrifugal energy of our own creations, reproduced and repeated again and again by the subconscious Moon.

If Leo, its ruler the Sun, or the analogous house – the fifth – are emphasised in a chart, the dot within the circle, or the lion, are relevant metaphors for whatever may be going on in that person's character or in their life.

The difficulty is that metaphors do not mean anything *"exactly"*. They give us clues. As there are many metaphors in a chart, the job of the astrologer is to be a Sherlock Holmes: we need to find the story or the stories in which all the clues make sense together.

Along Leonine lines, some people will boast about their ego, keep seeking attention and annoy everyone. They may be attention seekers who exclaim, like itchy dots at the centre of their circle: *"I am here! Look at me I am here!"* This attitude is not wrong. It's simply childlike.

"Look, Mum, I'm climbing this tree! Look at my drawing, Mum! Look, Mum, I jumped over the puddle! Look, Dad, I can ride my bicycle without the little wheels!"

We all need the light and warmth of loving attention to grow up, and keep emotionally healthy. A swollen ego that keeps seeking attention all the time is a wounded inner child. Swelling is the result of trauma.

On the other hand, Leo energy is also demonstrated by the one who provides this loving attention, as a parent or a role model.

They say *"Look!"* and instead of showing their ego, they show how things work, they share their lights, they lead by example, they teach and educate.

The best way to teach is to show how to learn, and the best way to learn is to play, to enjoy, to love whatever we're learning (which doesn't mean effort and will power won't be needed, but when you know what you love, you're much more likely to focus your effort and willpower).

Another way to educate is to let both children and adults alike believe you're just an entertainer. A clown, a storyteller, an actor, a writer, a director, a painter, a sculptor, a musician, a dancer... All teach, all show.

The smallest blade of grass teaches something to those who have eyes to see.

One of our favourite shows is romance. Real lovers show their naked bodies and souls to each other. Or at least we try. In the process, we enact the myth of Adam and Eve – suddenly ashamed of being just who they are, after eating the fruit from the tree of knowledge of good and evil.

It takes Leo courage to remove our fig leaves, our psychological defence mechanisms and unveil our wounds and vulnerability while announcing:

"Here I am!"

It takes Leo generosity to love the unveiled, vulnerable and wounded other, half-disgusting frog, half-charming majesty.

However, this story may well have to unfold within ourselves first. The Leo challenge is that the inner frog needs our own inner loving kiss. Our crippled sides need to come into the light and warmth of our own consciousness and be welcomed with the mercy and generosity of our own heart. This attitude is heroic, as it means breaking away from values which are both toxic and prevalent where we normally dwell, under the Moon.

When the frog within turns into a princess or a prince, it is free to kiss other frogs with genuine love but when there are only frogs to kiss frogs, the situation may be problematic.

Fortunately, there is a dot, a Source of love at the centre of the magic circle. Lion hearts are challenged to go there and radiate warmth and light, without waiting for someone else to do it first. This is true leadership. This is how we break curses.

Life is a sublime outpouring of magnificent energy!

31

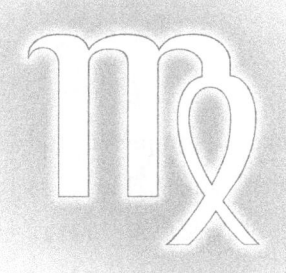

Virgo: Almost ready

To write this chapter, I had to make a list of topics. In the first draft the list served as an introduction. However, soaked in Virgo spirit, I couldn't help feeling dissatisfied, so I wrote it again and again. As I kept improving the organisation of this piece, it became clear that I couldn't fit everything in one single and coherent text.

Subtitles became necessary. Some topics on the list became subtitles, others were simply mentioned in the course of the explanations. Eventually, I was forced to abandon my attempt to explain everything with absolute clarity, so you'll have to make do with the best I can do for now.

Astrology is a language of symbols; it always opens new ways of understanding, and will never stop doing so. The list of topics or subtitles within the subject matter is infinite. There is no last word to God's creation. We have to accept our limits; humility is the only way to keep our peace of mind.

Virgo is the last sign of the first half of the zodiac

Summary of the previous chapters: Since Aries, the energy has been moving away from the centre. (♂) The centre is Spirit, or Source, or Tao. Away from Source we flow into existence. To ex-ist literally means to be out. To exist, the energy-spirit-consciousness wraps itself in bodies. There are various planes of existence. Earth is the element of the densest one: the material plane.

Virgo is associated with this element. We are spirits in the material world.

In Virgo whatever spirit is coming into existence is completed and perfected. We have already met the Earth element with Taurus. This sign means more specifically that after the initial impulse of Aries, the energy is becoming or acquiring substance.

Taurus doesn't go into details. Metaphorically speaking, before Taurus, there is no material, only energy, and after Taurus you get a heap of bricks. After Virgo there will be a building.

I am talking at a very abstract level. Of course, people born under the sign of Taurus have the reputation of being builders (not just hoarders of stuff). Human beings always live all the energies because they are so intimately intertwined in the fabric of life. People with a strong emphasis in Taurus will be more specifically attuned to the idea of giving or acquiring substance (materializing). Virgo is the sign that means organisation.

The signs are grouped in various ways. There are four series of three. Cardinal-Fixed-Mutable is the common pattern. The Cardinal signs give the tone, set the intention and initiate the movement. The energy is focused towards action. Fixed signs concentrate and stabilize. Mutable signs distribute the energy.

The first series: Aries-Taurus-Gemini tells the story of life along very broad lines. This series starts in Fire and we get the spirit without entering into details. Aries comes first: there is energy. What is most essential about Earth is that it is *substance*: with Taurus there is stuff we are made of. Then Gemini, an Air sign, brings the third ingredient: information. Energy, substance and information: all there is in the world is made of that. Notice that the Sun is exalted in Aries and the Moon in Taurus.

Now we are going to tell the story of life again, but this time there is an environment, a place in space and time from where to start. Roots have become possible. The second series starts with a feminine Yin sign, Cancer, ruled by the Moon; the story of life is now told in terms of formation. With energy, substance and in-formation, forms are created.

The Moon is Mother. The adventure starts in a nurturing environment, a womb, a cocoon, a matrix where life can grow. Cancer means both mother and child, as one can't exist without the other.

The Moon gives birth to the Sun.

In Leo is the *"Divine Child"*. The creator lives at the centre of the creature, the potter is alive within the clay. Leo means both child and parent, as one can't exist without the other. In Leo, the parents are the role models, they show the child how to express itself, through and beyond the form they have been given. The first parent to invite the child to live *beyond mother* is, rather logically, the father.

After Mother and Father, Virgo, the Virgin, is a young woman.

In Virgo, the creation of the body is perfected. Substance is organised. The body is an organism. Life is organic. In Virgo, incarnation is achieved.

Similarly, every time we create something (Leo), we end up immersed in details and organisation. We become servants of our own creative spirit.

Bodies are drawings. Spirit is the artist. Matter is the paint. Virgo is the tip of the paintbrush.

Virgo is alone.

Etymologically, "alone" comes from all one. The Great Spirit is all One in an absolute sense. "Before" Yin and Yang, there is no duality.

However, moving away from Source we perceive ourselves as separated conscious egos, Yahoo!!

The One plays at being many different beings. The individuation process culminates in Virgo. We are microcosmic works in progress.

We are ears of corn in the fields, we are becoming grains, beautifully aligned, hard, dry, unable to melt and merge... yet. We are egos. We are seeds. Everyone is one.

The zodiac is a cycle. The Moon and its phases are the archetype of all cycles. We can superimpose them.

Aries is like a New Moon, it's the starting point.

Just before the Full Moon, Virgo adds the final touch before completion. Virgo is individuality. Spirit-consciousness-energy has become an organic whole: It is one. It is *some one*.

It takes being one to meet another one. At zero-degrees Libra, the energy will be wearing a wedding dress.

The Virgin belongs to no man. She is almost ready. She has learned how to cook and heal. She knows how to deal with everyday life. The Moon is her mother, the Sun is her father. She is leaving them behind.

Before the wedding, the Virgin is alone.

Astrology is a symbolic language

Just in case... I hope you remember that astrology is a symbolic language. The message of Virgo is not about teenage girls having to refrain from sexuality, no more than Libra means that you have to be officially and religiously married to be with someone. You can follow your own traditions and opinions for these matters.

Symbols describe life. If the psyche wishes to convey "one who is not united to another one" it will display the symbol of a virgin. This can mean "before union" in the context of a union to come.

Every woman and every man is a virgin before their first kiss.

She brings an ear of corn. Again, it's a symbol. We can think of all the work that has been done, from ploughing the fields to harvesting to obtain this ear of corn. Then we'll be going to the mill for grinding and with the flour we will make bread. Virgo is showing transformation after transformation. Virgo's glyph looks quite like Scorpio's.

Bread is a symbol; it means food on the table. Behind the ear of corn we see work, *the daily grind*, we see life skills, including professional ones.

The medicinal plant, similarly, shows knowledge about body maintenance and health. When the Virgin masters that which is symbolised by the two plants she carries, she is a grown up. She doesn't need her parents to support her anymore. She is ready to get married. Maybe she won't. She is independent.

When a life cycle successfully reaches a Virgo phase, our body, mind and spirit are well aligned. If not, our organization falls apart. We may worry and feel pain in the gut. Virgo rules over the intestines, the place where food is broken down into small components and assimilated by the organism or eliminated. Sorting out, differentiating, discriminating are typical of Virgo activities.

An organism is a living organisation. Every organ has a place and a function. No organ wants to beat another organ or take its place. No organ wants all the blood for itself alone. Being humble is knowing one's place. So, in the body, so in nature and so in society. What is health?

When we can't digest our experiences, coping mechanisms turn into bad habits or compulsive rituals; life becomes a mess. Our physical and mental health may deteriorate. We become a nervous wreck. We may need the help of a therapist to analyse ourselves. To analyse is to look into the details of our thoughts, actions and memories and thoroughly discriminate.

The way we lead our life is a reflection of the state of our mind – or soul. Are we self-contained and well-integrated within ourselves? Are we dissociated, possessed by conflicting urges, at war with ourselves, possessed by hubris? What kind of partner would we be then?

"I am the Lord's servant", said a famous virgin. The Lord is the Heart. His rule is sweet.

32

Libra: Balance is stronger than strength

I like to think that the scales were handed over to Libra by Virgo. My grandmother used them to measure the correct amount of flour, butter or other ingredients for cooking. Airy Libra uses them as a symbol.

Libra's life lesson goes like this:

Not enough, let's add a little bit... Still not enough, let's add a little bit more... Not enough... It's too much now!!! ... A little bit less... Too much less! A little bit more again, but not as much as before... Yes, that's it!

The two pans seem to be gently floating in the air as the handle in the middle slowly settles into a perfectly vertical position, as vertical as a sword in the hand of a beautiful woman; she is as beautiful as the Virgo virgin, she looks more serious though, standing straight above the portal of a court.

Whoever sees the scales sees the sword. Libra is opposing Aries. They are the two sides of the same coin. The sword is action, the scales are decision making. Weighing up pros and cons, accusation and defence, desires and fears, merchandise and value, rights and duties, debit and credit, karma and gifts.

The scales are held by Osiris. On one side, a human heart. On the other side, a feather. Lightness is our ideal.

Libra is a Latin word meaning both *"balance"* and *"pound"*, a unit of weight. In French, the word *"balance"* (same spelling, charmingly different pronunciation) means *"the scales"*.

The English word *"balance"* translates in French as *"équilibre"* a word made of *"equi-"* meaning *"equal"* and *"libre"* which of course comes from *"libra"*: balance is same weight.

The British pound or the pound sterling is called *"livre sterling"* in French.

In the British monetary system *"sterling"* was the official measurement of quality for the silver or gold used for coins. *"Sterling"* also means *"high quality"*.

With the sterling Libra, you measure quantities with quality. Venus rules. It's official.

Look at the good old scales. Observe the handle in the middle turning into a spine and the pans into hips. When walking all the weight goes on one leg whilst the other moves forward, and then the law of justice says that it's the other leg's turn to bear the weight whilst the one moves forward. Libra rules the lower back and the kidneys. The centre of gravity is surrounded by Aphrodite's magic belt. Walking becomes dancing. Lightness is our ideal. It's very sexy.

First of the second half

In astrology, we're working with the principle that what comes first defines the totality of what comes next. That's why we keep looking at birth charts. Libra is the first sign of the second half of the zodiac.

The whole zodiac is an Aries story, an adventure called individuation. In Virgo, the sign of the maiden that belongs to no man, independent existence reaches a peak.

After Virgo, we will experience the throes and delights of union, from one-to-one relationships to sinking in the ocean of Piscean ecstasy. From now on, every sign we'll meet will be the polar opposite of a sign we already know. Every *"I"* will become part of a *"We"*.

Libra: Balance is stronger than strength

Libra is also the second Air sign on the wheel. Gemini came first to create links with no strings attached, only little wings at Mercury's feet. Libra binds. Venus dances with you. On one pan of the scales, you get more company, on the other, less freedom.

Libra is also the second Venus ruled sign in the zodiac. Venus Taurus is glue. When lovers almost literally eat each other, when two merge into one sensual flesh soaked in oxytocin, when they whisper or shout *"I am yours!"* or *"you are mine!"*, we are on the Taurus-Scorpio axis. Venus Taurus is a mouth or a vagina. She is Earth, she is Yin, she takes in.

Venus Libra is a magnetic field. She operates in the Air. Her law is attraction. She binds from a distance, she casts spells, she enchants, she charms. When a beautiful princess appears, admirers become satellites. As much as she dreams of the ideal relationship, she may love the status quo, content to keep as many of them in her orbit as possible and never commit. She is in no hurry to grow old.

Once upon a time, a princess declared that she would marry only the man who would bring her one hundred dragon heads still steaming... In many tales various impossible tasks have to be carried out for a guy to deserve her hand, and they all fail. One day however, a hero hears of the princess. The impossible guy will put an end to her indecision.

One upon another time, there was a satellite that was so attractive that the princess lost her balance and became a satellite of that very satellite. No one was at the centre, only relationship was. Relationships always happen *in between*. Mars is in exile and the Sun is in fall in Libra. Hiya Barbie! Hi Ken!

Marriage is the archetype of all associations, be they formed with or without official proceedings and ceremonies. There are always contracts however: when you enter a relationship, without knowing it, you sign up for a whole set of unwritten rules.

When we don't discuss the terms and conditions of our relationships consciously, we do set the rules subconsciously. A good deal simply consists of conforming to social customs about gender roles, society's expectations, the way things are done...

It's the simplest way. Libra is one of the most conformist signs, along with Capricorn. I feel tempted to say that all couples are the same. I may be biased, but do you know many eccentric couples? I mean eccentric in the way they relate to each other. You can dress up in a very unique style but still the woman cooks and the man puts up shelves.

Let's be nuanced. There is still room for specific rules for each couple. Who decides on what? Who is the boss, who opposes resistance, who just does what the other wants simply to keep the peace? Who suggests new ideas, who bothers about logistics, who listens more? How long is it OK to do something on your own without picking up the phone? Why is it fine to invite a friend to eat without notice when it's your friend, but not when it's mine? Who initiates sex, what is the rhythm of things? What's the balance of power? What is fair?

When they get into Scorpio, the partners may realise that they just assumed they were on the same wavelength. If they were not, they may divorce, those who once loved each other become enemies; they go to court to sort out who keeps the house, what will be going on with the children and who will pay and how much.

Above the portal, Lady Justice, scales in one hand and sword in the other whistles in Libra rising style, "Oops, I did it again!"

Marriage is the archetype or all one-to-one associations. Businesses can get married, best friends are couples, countries sign alliances and trade deals, atoms lose their freedom and form molecules...

There is always one side and another side, always a bond between the two and then the eternal question of finding the right balance.

A bit of mathematics

I like to say that symbols are magical doors. Each time you pass through one you may enter a new landscape. The scales can present an image of hips engaged in the activity of walking, limping or dancing, or a man and a woman falling in love, a court of justice, two business men signing a contract... We really need to know the context, or be very intuitive.

Let's open the Libra door again. On one pan, something. We don't know what it is. On the other pan, something else. We don't know what on earth it might be either.

However, what we know for sure is that there is a particular relationship between these two unknown things: their weights – symbols of all measures – are either equal, or one is heavier than the other. To keep it short, I'll call the weight of the unknown thing on one side "x", the weight of the other unknown thing "y". If they are equal, I'll just write $x = y$, if they are not, it may be that $x < y$ or $x > y$.

All the universe of mathematics is opening in front of us: we are now talking relationships in the abstract. It's so beautiful I want to cry!

Dane Rudhyar says that astrology is the algebra of life.

By the way, two quantities are in the golden ratio if their ratio is the same as the ratio of their sum to the larger of the two quantities, expressed by the formula: $a + b / a = a / b$.

Venus rules. Beauty is a question of proportions.

In the Air we imagine ideals, perfect forms, harmonies of colours and shapes, nuances of tones, elegance and movements. The beauty and harmony we create as artists or enjoy is the result of an inner sense of measure, the ability to sense the right amount of everything. We feel a little bit disgusted at how gross everyday reality is when compared to art and how could we not compare when under the influence of the scales? Libra folks are appalled when Fire signs fart and laugh in their face.

On the material plane weights are objective measures, but enter the psychological realm and they become subjective values. It's complicated. What is the weight of an argument, how light or heavy is a feeling?

If a man works hard and earns good money to pay the bills, does that weigh the same as cooking, cleaning, watching the kids and making sure there is always cold beer in the fridge?

What is fair and what is not, when everyone measures according to standards that vary in line with personal tastes and feelings and at the same time are influenced by social norms?

Everyone carries their own scales within, but only God knows what is the absolute weight of our soul. No one outside of us knows how we experience life. Something can be a deep pain for one person and not that hard for another, but if what shows on the outside is similar, who can tell the difference?

A nice little conclusion

I hope I managed to get the message across: with symbols, it's not possible to have a simple and clear definition. When it comes to character traits, Libra people have a reputation of struggling with decision making and can be prone to hesitating indefinitely. It is often true. This goes with understanding other people's point of view so well they forget to have a personal one. There are other ways to dysfunction though. Another one is to systematically play Devil's advocate: Libra feels the need to balance one-sided views with opposite opinions.

Sometimes Libra people have strong views and fight for justice with determination. Sometimes they are desperately seeking to solve inner conflicts and sometimes they have a knack for balance, great taste and wonderful social skills.

A chart is an architecture of metaphors. Ask the context for clues and be nice.

33

Scorpio: Holding on and letting go

Scorpio is the other side of Taurus.

Taurus rules over the throat, vocal cords and neck. In this Venus-ruled sign, we add substance to the initial impulse born in Aries.

When our body does Taurus, adding substance is eating. When our wallet does Taurus, adding substance is earning money. When our sense of self-worth does Taurus, we take in compliments. There is always guaranteed substantial growth for your capital with bull energy.

The opposite of input is output. We are tubes. At one end we eat and drink, at the other we piss and shit. This reality is hilarious. (How old is your inner child?) Even if we think we have outgrown pee and poo times, we have strong emotional roots in that mud.

It's worth noticing that following the feminine signs is a journey through the digestive tract:

After Taurus, the next Yin sign, Cancer, rules over the stomach. Then comes Virgo and the intestines. The glyph of Virgo looks like meandering bowels.

Then Scorpio appears. It is ruled by Mars and we push things out. The glyph looks like Virgo's but with a different ending.

If you're an ecologist and very fond of the wonderful recycling cycles of Mother Nature, you won't be shocked if I tell you that our corpse is, in a way, our excrement. It is substance that no longer serves us. We leave it behind as a gift to the earth, it will become humus, feed plants and one day the nutrients will find their way back onto other people's plates with renewed vitality. However, for the dying ones and their loved ones, it feels like a big loss.

We are all on the same journey and, at some point, we will find our way to the other side of the famous veil. Death is a fascinating reality for those born with Scorpio emphasis.

Continuing on our journey through the feminine signs, after Scorpio, only the bones, ruled by Capricorn, will defiantly resist decomposition. Archaeologists in a distant future may unearth them and call us Lucy.

Ultimate dissolution and return to spiritual unity are symbolized by the two fish swimming in opposite directions and next, we will be incarnating again in Taurus.

Scorpio rules over death. There are many types of death, the physical one being a symbol for many other deaths which all consist of "leaving behind".

It's not always easy. We often have to grieve, like a little girl I knew. She wanted a new haircut. She really wanted it. It would make her so pretty! This little princess had beautiful long hair. After it was cut, she looked into the mirror and burst out in tears.

There is no change without loss, loss is inevitable, nothing is permanent. However, the tears of a little girl in front of the mirror are infinitely respectable, and ours are futile on the way to the graveyard.

Taurus is gain; Scorpio is loss. It is not possible to refrain from dying. Life passes through us like a river. We assimilate lessons, digest experiences and release what needs to be released, spontaneously or, on occasion, with the help of a good shaman-therapist-exorcist. We need to get things out.

As children we learned to control these things getting out of our bodies. When we were two years old, we found out how to keep the stuff inside, under our control, for a certain amount of time, and to let it out only at the right place - that is, on the potty.

Meanwhile, we also learned to say *"No!"*. We were terrible twos. That's what being anal is about: we were experimenting with power. No, I won't let my poo escape now. No, I won't eat my soup. No, I won't submit to your law. No, I won't tell you where the rebels are hiding. My power. Fuck off.

Scorpio: Holding on and letting go

Scorpio is ruled by Mars, the warrior, and it's a feminine sign. In masculine Aries, Mars is projecting its aggressive and assertive fire from inside out. In feminine Watery Scorpio, the warrior is on the sensitive receiving end, enduring and keeping it all inside: the fear, the pain, the desire to fall onto the ground and cry like a baby, the terror and the rage, the urge to shit one's pants.

The warrior is keeping all his feelings inside. He looks impassive like Clint Eastwood chewing a cigar under the sun of a spaghetti western.

In a more 'peace and love' fashion, Scorpio energy pushed to the extreme becomes Jesus Christ on the cross. He was tortured to death and was still speaking with fixed determination the same words of love and forgiveness as he did when he could breathe freely.

Less glorious but essentially similar experiences are our lot. We are nailed to the cross of matter. Fears, passions, desires and frustrations, shame, guilt, rage and dark feelings test our souls. Holding in or letting go? We are a battlefield. Demons and angels fight for the throne. (It's symbolic language).

Demons are instant gratification monkeys. If they are hurt, they want to hurt. If they are scared, they want to kill. If they feel frustrated, they want revenge. If they feel ashamed or guilty, they search for scapegoats to make them feel how they feel. Expect bullies, inquisitions and holocausts.

Wise angels don't deny the need for releasing, as the suffering is real, but it has to happen with consciousness, at the right place and time, without causing harm. Becoming able to cry is one way.

Scorpio is this inner battle. When demons win, the outcome is dirty. When angels surround the throne, peace reigns and it smells like heaven. There is no victory without deep transformation. There is death and rebirth in the process.

Male sexuality also has to develop the strength of holding in and the power of letting go at the right moment. Premature ejaculation is a failure to control excitation. Erectile dysfunction is the counterpart: an erection, paradoxically, happens when some muscles relax. If they don't, the thing remains a bit too soft to please. The causes may be physical but they are often emotional, and have, without a shadow of a doubt, great emotional impact. Feelings about self-worth are at stake.

I may have had direct experience of female sexuality in other incarnations but I won't go into details about how it feels.

However, I can say that between men and women the whole game of holding in or letting go is re-enacted. Attraction and desire are powers, they are opportunities to play games. If one can't help running, the other will make them run. If one can't let go and become vulnerable, the other won't open up.

Sexuality is emotional intimacy. If we were all innocent, free from anything we would rather hide, then being partners would be the simplest and happiest thing in the world. But once Venus attracts and glues two humans to each other, the whole of themselves, not only their very valued sides, are joined... How will they deal with the complicity of their shadows? Egos have to die.

From birth to death, we need to find just the right balance of holding in and letting go, of controlling and going with the flow. This is important like life and death, important like a night of love worth remembering forever, important like living proudly with all our shit together.

And of course, we don't have it all together, hence all the drama.

34

Sagittarius: Where is the grail?

Times are prehistoric. There are no cars, no planes, no trains. The shaman can fly when he or she dreams and see where the animals are. Following the shaman's instructions, breeders or hunters go half-running, half-walking.

One day, someone had the idea and the audacity to climb on a horse. Humans found out that they could go much faster, much further away, explore the landscapes beyond the horizon and come back in no time. Imagine the exhilaration!

Some fell so in love with their mounts that they spent most of their lives riding them. They loved the great power between their thighs. Horse and rider became one creature. Centaurs made their appearance in the fantasy world.

Cattle breeders became cowboys. Hunters and warriors became skilled at shooting arrows whilst riding. Yahoo!

Do you remember when you learned to ride a bicycle? That power coming from your thighs, Sagittarius rules it. You were able to go faster, further away and explore. How do you think a jet pilot feels? Sagittarius is the sign for that.

Everything is relative. If you're a baby and most of your life is spent stuck in a cradle, Sagittarius energy is expressed when you start moving around on your hands and knees and threaten to fall down the stairs. My little brother did just that. I saw him from below bouncing like a ball on the cement steps of the staircase to the cellar. I should have closed the door, but I was a kid as well. He was fine. Sagittarian luck I suppose.

When baby is a bit older, moving around the house becomes familiar. It's Gemini connection. Sagittarius is always aiming further away, outside the house, on the other side of the busy road or into the next borough...

If baby doesn't stop, one day he or she may jump into the void in a wingsuit, go down glaciers on a mountain bike, live with indigenous people in the wilderness... There are risks. That's exciting. It's part of the game. Fear doesn't help, so why live in fear? Have faith!

Mercury is in exile in Sagittarius. If you travel to faraway places with a rudimentary grasp of local languages and you encounter customs that are completely alien to you, communicating will be a challenge. Little journeys into the jungle are as easy as going to the shop next door for the local people, but not for you!

Mercury is in domicile in Gemini. The twins are two but these two are the same. Mutual understanding is facilitated when you stand on common ground.

From physical exploration to knowledge and wisdom.

The more you explore the unknown, the more you learn. The more you learn, the more you know.

The more you know, the more there is to know.

Knowledge is an ever-expanding world! You may claim that all you know is that you know nothing, and still this wise Socratic admission of ignorance means that you know more than the random person in the street.

Explorers become researchers, guides, scholars, teachers... Literally or metaphorically, they keep drawing maps of new territories – they don't have time for details, they are busy enough with broad outlines. Gemini and Virgo will finish the job for them.

Librans think Sagittarians say *"I know"* a little bit too often, and that they should get down from their high horse, take off their muddy boots, shower and change when invited in for a cup of tea. Librans don't want to offend, so they keep inviting the centaurs into the China shops. They know it's a mistake but they don't know how not to do it. Too bad!

Sagittarius is mutable Fire.

Aries is intense focus, moving forward in one direction. Leo is central power, a king sitting on a throne, radiating. Sagittarius expands this power. It moves forward like Aries but in all directions at the same time, like an empire pushing its borders further North, East, West and South. Yes, that's the perfect recipe to end up spreading yourself too thin. Fortunately, human beings have some Saturn and enough of the Earth element to keep themselves grounded and look after logistics, but that's another story.

Mutable signs bring the unfolding of their element to the ultimate conclusion. Ruled by the Mercury-Jupiter polarity, they learn all there is to learn. After them, new beginnings will follow. They conclude.

Fire is spirit, it's our most intimate identity, the very essence of our being. Aries jumps on stage and fights for a place. The show goes on with Leo holding the space: this is who I am!

Sagittarius takes some distance and wonders. *"But who am I?"* Or *"What am I?"* The centaur embarks on a philosophical journey, a quest for Truth. Being is great and consciousness wants expansion.

Let's have a second look at the Centaur. I was so pleased with myself when I realised that this imaginary creature was expressing what horse riders experience – being one with their mount – that I could have developed the tendency to dismiss any other interpretation. Dogmatism is a trap for truth seekers. Symbols are multifaceted.

What if the picture of a centaur – the torso of a man, the body of a horse – was a description of a process of transformation?

A horse is turning into a human. The animal nature has lost the head – it doesn't lead anymore. For the rest it is still what it is, bottom, legs, body, instincts.

Whinney!!! Where is my head?

Above nature is super-nature. Culture has its roots in nature and its branches in the supernatural.

What is a human being? The Centaur asks the same question as the Sphinx – another mythical creature made of animal parts and a human head.

"What animal walks on four legs in the morning, on two legs at noon and on three legs in the evening?" the Sphinx asked Oedipus. The question is indeed much deeper than the mere riddle it seems to be. *"Man"* is the answer. *"What is man?"* is the real question.

We are supernatural beings. We are spirits in the material world. We are horses turning into humans turning into...? We'll see!

Left to itself, the horse would graze, go to water and drink, reproduce with enthusiasm, flee from danger and that would be it. Many humans don't do much more than horses. A few ask questions. What's the meaning of all that? Can we improve nature, can we change? Do we have free will? Did I hear a call from above?

A great struggle with our animal nature took place in Scorpio, the sign usually associated with the word *"transformation"*. The picture of a scorpion is similar to a skull with two crossed shin bones. The old being dies, the new being is born.

Where shall we go after we die? In Sagittarius! Full of life, we will be running forward, aspiring upward. With strength and concentration, the human half will turn into a spiritual arrow, a will to reach heaven.

Shooting arrows at the sky is praying. Jupiter, the Lord of Sagittarius, *Zeus* in Greek, from the Indo-European *Dyeus*, the sky father, answers prayers turning the cornucopia of divine abundance down and showering the faithful with benedictions. Praise the Lord, Hare Krishna, Hallelujah, Amen.

Where is the Grail?

35

Capricorn: Don't separate the fish from the goat

The first eight signs of the zodiac looked rather ordinary. The word *"zodiac"* etymologically means *"The wheel of animals"*.

We have met a ram, a bull, human twins, a crab... The scorpion was scary but still grounded in known reality. Then a centaur made its entrance, and now a sea goat. This thing can neither swim nor climb. It can't remain the same. What is shown here is a fish turning into a goat. It's us.

The fish is the state we're leaving behind, the goat is what we are becoming but we're not fully there yet.

We shouldn't be too radical with the idea of leaving behind. The fish lives in the water, which symbolises our feeling nature. Getting rid of our emotions and sensitivity altogether would make us heartless robots.

Jung noticed that the unconscious and the conscious are in a relationship of compensation. I should have mentioned this when talking about Libra! If our conscious attitude is characterised by too much of a certain thing, the unconscious will adopt a too-much-in-the-opposite-direction attitude.

Jung gave the example of a patient he had not much esteem for. In a dream, this patient appeared on top of a high tower, far above him; Jung realized he was being unfair. Had he idealized his patient, he may have dreamed of her wallowing in the mud instead.

We shouldn't be literal when interpreting symbols. A fish turning into a goat does not mean everything fishy in our nature has to become goaty. We just need to become a little bit more like the goat.

In childhood and maybe before incarnating we were like fish in the sea, immersed in the universal or maternal soul, not knowing the difference between the atmosphere of our environment and our internal state. If one or two babies start crying in a nursery, soon all of them are crying. They have no idea why. They just absorb the vibe and amplify it.

Join an emotional crowd at a political rally and you'll feel the power. You can feel it on social media as well. Current trends and fashions pass off as personal opinions, but it's nothing but the sea. Sometimes it feels good and reassuring. Sometimes, tossed around by the flows, we crave for an island, we want a strong and independent ego.

Let's not confuse the ego with flaws such as pride, arrogance or selfishness. Ego means literally *"me"*. Children who fail to build a healthy sense of being a "me" become psychotic or at least will spend a good deal of their life struggling with issues of personal boundaries. They will not know what they want, not know what to do with themselves. They will be labelled *"personality disorders"*.

The ego that is stigmatised by spiritual teachings is not the ego itself, but its excesses, which may at times be reproached by Capricorns – but only when they are Capricorning too far.

The fish turns into a goat, the sea turns into a mountain. Rocky slopes won't carry the animal to the top like ocean currents offering fish a ride to the other side of the sea. Our Mamas won't carry us forever. Climbing rocks will make us strong. It's a straight, uphill and narrow path that leads to the kingdom of heaven.

Capricorn is Cancer's polarity. The crab has already started getting out of the sea. Crabs run on the shores when the tide is low. Fish don't do that. Children explore their surroundings, they are safe, their parents are watching. Children can run back to safety near their parents whenever they feel the need. Is there someone watching over the parents?

Adulthood can be a lonely place. Vigilance is the old-fashioned term for mindfulness. A goat perched high on a rocky mountain ledge can't afford to escape reality drifting into absent mindedness. Crying for help won't help either.

Capricorn: Don't separate the fish from the goat

In spirit we remain children of heaven and earth. To remember this, we have to climb the sacred mountain. The flesh may decay but we are invited to the safety of an eternal dwelling. However, there is no way around it, we need to do some climbing by ourselves.

My favourite master said:

"Unless you change and become like little children, you will never enter the kingdom of heaven."

The road to childlike simplicity *again* is upward. Striving to stand on their own two feet, reaching out to something higher than themselves is what children do.

Climbing is not always climbing the sacred mountain. More often than not, it's on the social ladder that we are struggling our way up from bottom to top. Is it a perversion or preliminary training?

Sometimes, it's on the neck of a guitar or in the ring, on a stage or behind the wheel that we're trying hard to be on top of our game. Each time we strive to master something we are learning to master ourselves.

Saturn, ruler of Capricorn, is an energy of crystallisation. The process goes from wet to dry, from fish tail to goat horns and hooves. There is salt in the sea. In salt marshes, water evaporates, salt turns to crystals. It's dry and structured.

The potter makes pots and sculptures with wet clay. Once dry, the shape is fixed. Brick walls and terracotta plates aren't flexible – and that's a good thing.

In the womb, once the spermatozoa have met the egg, our body took form in water. Once shaped enough, we were born into a drier environment. We were still very soft when babies, even our bones were still elastic. The older we get the stiffer we become.

As children we absorbed our environment. We had an incredible memory, but not much mental stability. We were rather gullible and inexperienced. The older we become, the more we know what we ourselves think and want.

Crowds are ruled by the Moon. Put a lot of people together and you get an amorphous environment in which emotions and fanciful theories spread like pandemics.

When the time comes to elect leaders, candidates compete to win over public opinion with a tiny percentage of sound reasoning and a lot of communication techniques designed to impress public imagination. I would love to believe in anarchy, but it seems to me that children need parents and crowds need rulers.

Rulers are ruled by Capricorn.

Adults are rulers of themselves.

Capricorn is cardinal. It is the entrepreneur of the zodiac. The first steps are the more difficult ones. With this energy, we crystallise our intentions and resolutions into a relatively disciplined course of action. Efforts don't sound like fun? They can be though. There are great rewards, and in any case, too rigid a goat falls in the void.

"Nothing in excess" always applies.

Capricorn is a feminine sign. There are six axes in the zodiac. Three of them are made of Fire and Air signs, and the other three are Water and Earth signs. In the Western tradition, Water and Earth are feminine while Air and Fire are masculine. Feminine in this context means receptive, a builder of forms and bodies, with the purpose of manifesting on the material plane the spiritual seeds that have fecundated them.

Masculine means emissive, spiritual, immaterial, initiating.

We can switch to Taoist terminology and use Yin and Yang instead of masculine and feminine if this bothers your sense of social justice. However, when we come across figures like the young maiden called Virgo, or the muscular sexy guy pouring water from a jug symbolising Aquarius, we see male and female figures, so we should remember that there is a symbolic dimension at a deeper level than current polemics over gender issues.

Water and Earth are both feminine and opposed. The opposition of masculine and feminine being the archetype of all oppositions, we can understand Earth as the masculine in the feminine and Water as the feminine in the feminine.

Symmetrically, Air can be understood as the feminine in the masculine polarity, and Fire the masculine. Like Yin and Yang, these are relative values.

Saturn, ruler of Capricorn, symbol of authority and structures, at times interpreted as father, is a feminine energy, because it is focused in the form.

Mothers are not always nurturing and all-forgiving creatures. Children have to go to bed at night, get up in the morning, brush their teeth, eat fruit and vegetables, refrain from hitting their little sister with a hammer on the head, the list of musts and must-nots is a long and unavoidable one. Tough love is the Capricorn side of being a mother, with or without a father's help. There must be rules and boundaries.

Parents become masculine when, as role models, they shine like the Sun.

In the body, the densest tissues are the bones. They are inflexible. We need joints. Capricorn rules the skeleton and more specifically the knees, and also the skin for its role as a boundary.

Kneeling means submitting to the higher power you're asking to marry you. Responsibilities galore in store.

36

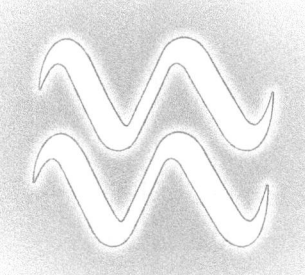

Aquarius: Fixed Air, really?

Isn't the idea of *"Fixed Air"* a little bit funny?

"Fixed" suits Taurus so well. Taurus has a justified reputation for inertia. Once it's somewhere, it stays there and becomes bigger, denser, fleshier... If Taurus moves, it acquires momentum: it gets settled in an unchanging motion.

"Fixed Fire" is easy to understand. At first, Fire feels cardinal. It is active, creative, energetic, initiating... Fixed fire manifests as central power. A king on a throne, a bonfire and the sun are radiating in all directions.

Water doesn't feel fixed at all. Water feels mutable. Dissolving, changing and merging, Pisces is as mutable as you can get. Water is formless, sometimes river, sometimes sea, mist, fog, cloud or rain, sometimes groundwater found deep down at the bottom of wells.

Here we are! In the desert, where scorpions live, water is deep down. Finding it is a question of life or death.

Wells, ponds, stagnant waters are fixed.

Three modalities, four elements, is it a game of musical chairs? Let's not confuse similarity with equivalence!

Air has a claim for being associated with the mutable modality. Fluid like Water and far more subtle, how could Air be fixed?

My ancestors were called the Gauls; they were afraid of only one thing: that the sky might fall on their heads. It never happened. Winds, birds and breathing evoke movement; Air finds fixity in infinity. The sky has no limit, is not contained, has no centre and doesn't move.

Air is space. Thanks to science we know that the atmosphere doesn't extend as far as the stars, but symbols are not concepts. They are fingers.

When the sage points at the Moon, the fool looks at the finger. When the finger is Air, the astrologer looks at the sky. The vault of heaven is everywhere and beyond, all the time and for ever after. And so are we – spiritual, infinite and eternal.

Fire and Air oppose each other. Aquarius and Leo are like sky and sun. One travels through the other and fills it with warmth and light. The other is the abode of stars and planets, and at times, of clouds, the water carriers. Aquarius is the water bearer. If the Sun shines in Leo, expect rain in Aquarius.

For farmers in the suburbs of Babylon, ancient Mesopotamia, the big muscular guy pouring out water from a jar on his shoulder was blessing the fields. Dance people dance! You will eat! Gather and express gratitude as a community!

Solidarity and cooperation have always been questions of survival. When life is difficult, you don't build as many irrigation systems as there are families in the village. You build one all together, and every individual farmer plugs themselves into it. There must be collective agreements. How do we share responsibilities and benefits?

There are disagreements, debates and procedures involved in decision making. Instincts don't rule over all behaviours; therefore, politics are unavoidable. Have you heard of the role of friendship in Aristotle's political theory?

Anyway. When it rains, you praise the sky gods and check the reservoirs.

From Earth to Air, concrete experiences become understanding in the abstract. Fields are now of activity and knowledge. Physics, economics, energy, biology, urban environment... Whatever your field, even if you've made a name for yourself thanks to your unique genius and original approach, you are not alone sowing and ploughing it. Human endeavours are collective. Life is a web.

However, as you sow, you reap, at a personal level and collectively. The articulation between the individual and society has been providing food for both thought and conflict since the beginning of thinking and arguing.

The Water Bearer doesn't represent the clouds, all the clouds and nothing but the clouds. Symbols are fingers, so let's go for a walk with our eyes looking upwards. Let's cross a busy road without even noticing. Don't we look like a stereotypical Aquarius, lost in our thoughts, oblivious to the realities which others take for obvious, focused on wider realities? Visions, ideals, equations, constellations, patterns, manifestos, divine architecture and rage, rage against the dying of the light...

(Dylan Thomas was a Scorpio Sun with Jupiter and Uranus in Aquarius setting on the horizon.)

The sky is as vast as the point at the centre of the circle which means *"The Sun"* is small: infinitely vast, infinitely small. We're high. We're gliding...

We're contemplating the immutable laws of the course of the stars, the perfect cosmic order underlying the apparent chaos of human life. Even revolutions kick off when the time is right, and mysteriously, free will is part of the equation. What wonderful clockwork!

Air is Yang. It shows the other side of the creative coin. Heads or tails? Fire is power. Air is idea. Whatever becomes manifest started in the spiritual dimension. Architects draw plans before any building work can start. Life has its architects. Ideas come first. Thoughts progressively become concrete realities. That's progress. The new wants to take the place of the old. The old can't help but resist, the new must insist, there can only be thunderstorms and earthquakes ahead. Saturn with new plans is fighting Saturn's old structures.

Aquarius is the Capricorn of the future. As soon as revolutionaries get their way, they create new structures, write a new constitution and establish a new order which they hope is designed well enough to stand the test of time... Will they?

If our mental creations are coherent; if we don't wish for a thing and its exact opposite to be true at the same time; if the plans of our house don't look like a painting by M.C. Escher; if traumatic memories don't force our creative thoughts to wander in inextricable labyrinths, then our thoughts, hopes and wishes will come true.

Uranus was the first of the transpersonal planets to be discovered. The traditional system was so balanced, so perfect! It could not be improved, only disrupted.

The Sun rules over Leo, the Moon over Cancer, the five planets rule over two signs each, one masculine and one feminine. Why strip away Saturn from its masculine side, and Mars and Jupiter from their feminine sides? If Uranus resonates well with Aquarius, that's fine! Let's keep Saturn there.

Shouldn't there be a feminine side to Uranus? I'm just asking, but it would make sense. Uranus could rule over Capricorn as well; Neptune over Sagittarius and Pluto over Aries. Mars, Jupiter and Saturn wouldn't stop being what they are. But what does *"ruling"* mean exactly?

I like to think of the connection between planets and signs as sympathetic strings in a musical instrument. These are strings that you don't pluck. They make sounds when other strings are played on the same frequency, or on a frequency like an octave lower or higher which makes them resonate. From my point of view, Uranus is the higher octave of Saturn. Bah! I'm just thinking...

The glyph of Aquarius looks like waves, as in wavelengths and frequencies.

Invisible energies cause visible manifestations.

37

Pisces: The way up and the way down

The way up and the way down are one and the same.

— Heraclitus

I have been wondering why Pisces rules the feet.

Aries rules the head, Taurus the throat, Gemini the lungs and so on. Following the signs we scan the body from head to toe. Order feels good but fish don't have feet, so why rule over ours?

Let's go for a little barefoot walk. Let's feel how the earth feels. It's a sensitive and intimate touch.

Psychics and mediums who attune themselves with the most subtle energies need to keep grounded. Feet are plugs and anchors.

A fish goes up, a fish goes down. Branches grow up, roots grow down.

The way up and the way down are one and the same.

The last shall be first, and the first last

— Jesus

Towards the beginning of the Age of Pisces, the first Christians chose the fish as a secret symbol to recognise one another and escape persecution.

Jesus's story and teachings are a true Pisces textbook. Not all people born with Pisces prominent in their chart are Jesus, indeed far from it. Symbols don't show only the hero of the story, but all that goes with it: where there is a saviour, there are victims; where there is a healer, there are sick people; where there is a redeemer, there are fallen angels. Demons are spiritual beings too. A fish goes up, the other goes down.

Jesus said that he was the Messiah the Jews had been waiting for. They were waiting for a king. Instead, he was born in a stable, washed his followers' feet and ended up being crucified like a criminal.

He valued the poor and the outcasts; when his disciples asked who was the greatest of them all, he told them they had to become like little children to be able to enter the spiritual kingdom.

He kept turning established values upside down. I love Jesus.

> *That which is below is like that which is above, and that which is above is like that which is below, to perform "the miracles of one only thing".*
>
> – Hermes Trismegistus

Talking of turning upside down... With Capricorn we have been climbing to the top of a mountain. With Aquarius we have reached to the clouds and the stars, the infinite space where Spirit dwells. We can't get any higher, but as above, so below. The sky calls for a down-below counterpart: it is the ocean. What is high is also deep.

Above are winged creatures, angels or birds. Below are starfish. Above is spirit. Below is consciousness. It's a mirror. Consciousness can be enlightened or obscured. In modern terms we distinguish between conscious and unconscious, and it can be personal or collective, but it's all the psyche, the universal soul, the feminine counterpart of Spirit. We are immersed in it. Creatures of the psychic ocean, we are fish.

In Christian symbolism, Mary, Stella Maris, is the Star of the Sea. She was first called that because of a wrong translation of her name by a monk in medieval times, but it struck a chord. A mere error without psychic resonance would have been quickly forgotten.

In the psychic ocean are images. An almighty father with a beard, a virgin beauty with stars around her head standing over the sea, a wise and benevolent elephant, blue skinned gods dancing and playing the flute, to mention but a few. They move our hearts. There is an emotional dimension

Pisces: The way up and the way down

called devotion, or worship to spirituality. We borrow these words to express our most romantic feelings.

Artists, musicians and story tellers find inspiration from this sea. In an ideal world, there would be no distinction between sacred and profane art.

Some religions make abundant use of images, others forbid their use. They can be inspiring but also misleading.

The Great Spirit, as far as I can tell, has no gender, no beard, no lovely face and no blue skin.

> *When all the senses are stilled, when the mind is at rest, when the intellect wavers not, then, say the wise, is reached the highest state. This calm of the senses and the mind has been defined as yoga. He who attains it is freed from delusion.*
>
> – The Upanishads

Consciousness is a mirror, and I don't know why a particular kind of mirror is called psyche. If it started as a coincidence, again it has struck a chord.

Psyche can only mirror spirit well when she is still like the surface of a lake. When she is not, distorted views create illusions. They can be beautiful like a blaze of lights dancing with the waves, reflecting the one and only Sun above.

Sculpted by the Aquarian wind, waves usually forget that they are the ocean. We identify with our outer form and then fear that we will have to die.

But who is forgetting? Is it the wave, the ocean, or spirit reflected in psyche?

We are in a prison we call reality. Return to Source is a lonely path, it seems.

There are two fish swimming in opposite directions. They are bound together. They can't be separated. There is only one fish. But they are two.

Nuns, monks, hermits, solitary sailors and prisoners live in tiny cells. A fish is sacrificed. It becomes smaller and smaller as the other one expands to mystical dimensions. The cell can be a hospital room, a mental or physical disability, a stigma... Jupiter rules.

It is a collective game.

Others are mirrors.

Spirit is making faces in the mirror.

Sometimes we smile, a mirror smiles and we're happy. When we are happy, we smile...

Sometimes we paint war on our face. Who started it? The mirror? Now we are facing the enemy, we become enraged, we curse, we slaughter. For as long as mirrors keep mirroring what keeps appearing in the mirrors, we will be spiralling out of control, hoping for heaven, going to hell.

Free spirits at times appear and demonstrate how to stop waiting for the mirror to love first. It takes strength not to mirror. It takes spirit to start alternatives. It may look like turning the other cheek.

Dissolving energy

On this material plane, Saturn has crystallised the forms we created yesterday. When we try a new smile in the mirror, psyche keeps reflecting back the sad face we have been feeding it for so long. There is a delay between sowing and reaping. That's why we remain so easily trapped in karmic loops.

Patience etymologically means suffering. Taking suffering as a supreme value is a mistake. We just need patience to let the old forms dissolve. The purpose is bliss, love and peace. Pisces remembers paradise.

That's why Pisces can mean the one who suffers, the sacrificed, the victim, the scapegoat. The one who absorbs rather than reflects; the one who is forced – or willingly accepts – to take on themselves the sins of others – their shadows – and redeeming the energies holding them is the light of a purified and understanding compassionate consciousness, free from judgement and hatred.

Pisces: The way up and the way down

Of course, this energy, like all others, can miss the point. There is only a Virgo split hair between enlightenment and madness. Artificial paradises are attractive. Dissolving old fashioned morality opens the door to old fashioned perversions. It's always possible to replace an illusion with another illusion. I don't need to insist...

There is a Zen story. There were three cats. They were the best at getting rid of mice. The first cat was incredibly swift, like the hero in a Kung Fu movie. The second one was psychic. It always knew in advance what the mice would do. The third cat was just a lazy old cat sleeping all day long. The thing about this old cat was that wherever it was, there were no mice. We want to be this cat.

3

Value of the fast moving things in the astrological chart

Imagine a gathering of people who were all born on the same day – same month, same year, same century. You are one of them. It's your birthday – and theirs. The Universe has organized a party and here you are, nibbling, drinking and socializing with all these same birthday people.

All your Suns are in the same sign, and all your planets as well. Only the Moon, which travels over about twelve degrees during one day, can possibly be found in two different signs, but other than that all your placements are pretty much the same.

What's amazing though, is that you are all quite different. One has already taken up the role of *"life and soul of the party"* – is that you? Some seem to feel a little bit out of place, some are helping; some are asking others how they feel and others tell you what they think before you ask... Blame most of the differences on your rising signs!

The rising sign is actually only one of the magnificent four: Ascendant, MC, Descendant and IC, aka Cross of Matter. Four angles forming two axes: the horizon and the meridian.

In the chart, every planet touched by an angle of the cross becomes a dominant energy. As this cross takes just one day to complete a round of the zodiac, amongst this group you'll find people with Venus dominant, Pluto dominant, Saturn dominant, Sun, Moon, Mercury, Jupiter, Uranus, Neptune, Mars... all will be represented.

The Universe, in its great wisdom, has even thought that the cross of matter shouldn't look the same everywhere on earth. In your Know-Yourself party, those who were born not too far from the equator have a cross worthy of the name, with horizon and meridian forming a really square angle.

For those born far in the far North or far South however, their cross will look flattened, as if a giant had walked on the meridian. The MC-IC axis will be much closer to the Ascendant-Descendant axis than you would have expected. If you love geometry, let's talk about why it's like that another day.

Just imagine that you have a square aspect, let's say a Venus-Saturn square. Everyone in the room has it. For everyone, there is a conflict to solve between the urge to relate and the need to set boundaries, a conflict between yes and no, love and ego, union and personal structure... This conflict is actually something so universal that all human beings experience it. The difference is that everyone in your group has this conflict more specifically emphasised than the average human being, and it plays out in connection with the values of the signs in which Venus and Saturn are found.

You all have it, but some of you have an angle on Venus, others have one on Saturn, others not at all. As a result, the interplay between these two energies will be rather different depending on the individual.

The cross of matter is the skeleton of the whole house system. Planets won't be active in the same houses for everyone. This also induces great variations between individuals.

I could now tell you the same story again with a variation: the Universe is organizing a party with people who were born in the same month rather than on the same day. The planetary placements will still be very similar, only the Moon will have visited all the signs of the zodiac over this period. The Moon comes just after the cross of matter as an indicator of individual differences. And the same principle applies: as the Moon moves around, she conjuncts and aspects all planets. A conjunction is the strongest aspect, then we have major and minor aspects, and all can be exact, tight or loose.

Value of the fast moving things in the astrological chart

All this just to tell you this basic but extremely important principle: the quicker something moves, the more personal its meaning.

General things are like 'having a nose'. It's true for almost everyone. It's very important to have a nose, those who lost theirs at war can testify for it, but if your lover say that what they love about you is that you have a nose, you won't feel especially thrilled. If you are a lover complimenting, your beloved's nose has to be small, pretty, elegant or anything nice that is particular to them. The more specific your description of the admirable proportions of the sniffing device, the more impactful the compliment.

If you are reading a chart, the same principle applies. To be specific, focus on the quickest moving things: the Ascendant, the cross of matter, the houses, then the Moon and the Sun, (which are also important for being luminaries), then the other personal planets, Mercury, Venus, Mars, then the intermediary planets Jupiter and Saturn, and if nothing special has been noticed in connection with the transpersonal planets after having reviewed the quicker points, don't make a fuss about them.

(Transpersonal planets will be in a particular house, therefore their house placement says something particular; however, houses do not emphasise energies like angles or fast planets do when they make strong aspects to them, so they won't become dominant purely for being in a house.)

I have one final and very important thing to mention, before you wander off to try meditation instead of learning astrology: yes, having a nose is very important. So is having a heart, a brain, a liver, a central nervous system. If you are learning medicine, you have to learn anatomy. You will not start learning what is particular to such or such individual. Anatomy is about what is true for everyone.

A reason why many people can't go into depth when reading charts is that they don't know psychic anatomy. Venus in Sagittarius has exotic tastes, yes, that's great. Knowledge is a value, that's fine, but what do we do with it? What's the real problem? What kind of suffering is there and what can we do about it? How can we articulate the inner conflicts and aspirations of a person in a way that really helps? What can be changed, what must be accepted? What does it all mean?

We can't understand Venus in isolation. We need to understand how all the planets interact as an organism, at the level Dane Rudhyar calls *"generic"*, the level of what is true for everyone, before looking at particular charts.

If we know that someone has a fantastic nose, but don't know that for everybody the nose is associated with the sense of smell, how could we think of perfumes or wine tasting? We need to talk about what's specific and particular, but we need to understand what's universal before being able to do so.

Understanding the whole organism is understanding the laws of the universe.

Astrology is part of what has been called occult sciences or esotericism. As for the word *"psychology"*, etymologically it means *"knowledge of the soul"*. Before rushing into studying complex astrological techniques, we had better learn what we are made of.

...Let me briefly summarise: in a chart, the fastest moving things (cross of matter, luminaries, Mercury, Venus, Mars) are the most personal indicators. They emphasize the importance of whatever they touch. In this way we can understand what is particular to the person whose chart we are reading, in the context of what is true for everyone. And we need to know what's true for everyone.

A pretty nose anyway...

39

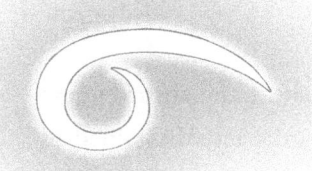

First things to look at

The first things to look at in a chart are the angles (Ascendant, MC, Descendant and IC) and the luminaries (Sun and Moon).

Here is a big fat principle that never fails: any planet conjunct one of these points is a major player.

For instance, in my chart, Saturn is conjunct the Descendant, the Moon is conjunct the IC, and Neptune is conjunct the Sun.

All the orbs are quite tight. It is relevant to start talking only about these three energies, what they are and, being what they are, how they are likely to interact.

There is no need to take our head in our hands and feel like our minds are about to explode. Yes, the planetary energies are deep and complex, and yes there is more to them than just a few easy key words, but let's start with something easy, and progress one step at a time.

Often, we don't see what is there, not because it is very subtle or complicated, but because it is so simple that we don't even notice it.

Here is something simple: Neptune dissolves boundaries, the Moon blurs them and Saturn creates or protects them. If you are a complete beginner, maybe you didn't know this? You know it now! We've just entered the labyrinth!

Neptune dissolves, the Moon binds emotionally, Saturn creates structures, limits and boundaries. Just thinking of this, we've found a major theme straight away: Jean-Marc has a problem with boundaries!

Please don't forget that I am talking about my natal chart and that I am fifty-eight years old at the time of writing. Yes, this has been a major issue, and no, it is not a curse. I have been working on it.

Magical Doors

When I was a rebellious teenager, I wrote a very short and absurd poem about a canal which was so narrow that the two banks actually joined in the middle and there was no room left for the water. This was an accurate description of my upbringing from a certain angle: too much structure is like no structure at all. Emotions can't be contained and channelled in this way. They can only overflow. In addition to Moon and Neptune being dominant energies, my Ascendant is Cancer, so for me Water comes first. Saturn being on the side of the Descendant will appear through others. I banged into a few walls.

As a result, I developed a strong tendency to withdraw into my shell, which is typical of Cancer.

I recall a conversation I had, in my youth, with a wise woman. She was an osteopath and had a deep understanding of human nature. She was not an astrologer. One day, after working on my spine, she explained to me that in the animal kingdom, less evolved creatures have their skeletons outside of their bodies: crustaceans, like crabs, have no backbone but a protective shell. More evolved animals and humans have a skeleton within, they can stand on their paws or feet and interact with the world through a more vulnerable but also more sensitive skin.

What I had to do, in her understanding, was to transition from an attitude which was more like the crustacean with an external protective shell to the human, who can be more open thanks to an internal skeleton.

I didn't know much about astrology at that time and she didn't know that I was Cancer rising with Moon and Neptune dominant, along with Saturn on the Descendant. She got the information directly from my body. (She was a Taurus).

I have been talking about myself, thanks for listening; you can forget about me now.

Remember this first principle:

Always look for planets at the angles or conjunct to the luminaries. There are often big things not to be missed there.

40

The worst way to interpret a chart

The worst way to interpret a birth chart is to ignore the fact that it is made of complex relationships and treat it merely as a list of placements.

If someone asks me: "I have Jupiter in Scorpio, what does that mean?" and if I happen to be in the mood, I answer with another question:

"I have put some emerald green in my painting, is it nice?"

Or, "I have composed a song and I've put a C minor chord in the middle of it, how does it sound?"

If a chart was a painting, the first question we should ask to describe it is: "What colour and what theme are dominant?"

That emerald green in the painting... is it a little dot in a corner, or does the whole picture look like a rain forest?

Does the painting look like a field of wheat below a blue sky with a weird but majestic white cloud in it, and a tall green cypress tree on the side? Or is it a bunch of multi-coloured flowers in a vase on a table?

In front of a chart, we need to get an idea of what kind of painting we're looking at.

We don't need long and convoluted explanations. If all we know is that there is some green in the picture, it may be the rain forest, or it could be a picture of a caravan of camels with long shadows walking in line in the desert and a few people walking alongside, one of them wearing emerald green pants.

I agree with you, only a little dot of green offsetting the overall sand tonality of the picture could bring something very special to the composition. However, it would still be something completely different to the festival of greenery seen in a rain forest.

Astrological charts are not less nuanced or complex than art and life.

That Jupiter in Scorpio in your chart, is it dominant? Is it on top of the list of the most important things to talk about? Or not?

Once we know which energies are the main players, we get a good enough idea of the big picture and our work of interpretation becomes relaxingly simpler.

Jupiter, as I've already mentioned, is the part of the mind who wants to see the broad lines, the frame, the whole. We need to tell Mercury to calm down a minute. But don't worry, the details are not lost. They will bring enlightening complements of information later.

41

Don't push the astro colours back into the tubes

You mix blue and yellow and you get green.

Green is not a shade of blue nor a shade of yellow, it's a different colour.

A painter, or anyone who loves colours, is able to look at a certain shade of green, and see the blue in it, or how akin this green is to the yellow spectrum.

Nevertheless, at the basic level, green is not blue, and green is not yellow.

In a similar fashion, we mix Sun and Moon signs, and of course the Ascendant and all our placements. The result of this mixing is our personality, and it's similar to the painter's palette. It's messy. In some places we can see original colours, in other places they blend in various ways.

The descriptions of the signs as character traits are what the painter gets when squeezing the tube.

The painting is what we are longing for, the reason why we keep mixing colours.

And to make things more exciting (or depressing according to the mood) for us, the palette, the painter and the canvas are only one thing.

Lists of character traits are useful as we need to understand the material, but identifying too much with our sign placements – as described in textbooks – is like trying to push the paints back into the tubes. It's not what we want.

42

How to understand Black Moon Lilith

First of all, there is the Moon. The Moon rules over our most sensitive life. She rules over intimacy.

When the Moon is visible at night, we are likely to be snuggling in a bed, cuddling or making love, sleeping, dreaming and enjoying the comfort of our home; sometimes we see the Moon during day time, but her glory rules the night.

She also symbolises motherhood and childhood, so let's feel vulnerable.

The Moon goes through phases and various cycles... She is sometimes closer to the Earth, and sometimes further away. Look at a one-year-old when their mum goes into the next room leaving them alone for a moment. They cry. They are scared. They feel abandoned. But Mother has to move away from them every now and then.

This is one of the great lessons we are forced to learn. She goes away, she comes back and again...

Psychologists, after Melanie Klein, know that we hate our mother when she "abandons" us. Then we feel scared and guilty of our destructive tendencies – we need her so much!

We love, we hate, we need, we fear, we crave. This is Black Moon Lilith.

We may reject what we most want, become cynical or guilty, ashamed and hateful, longing and craving... a key word is *"ambivalence"*.

Of course, we will use psychological defence mechanisms to bury her. She has gifts for us though. She offers a great initiation.

Magical Doors

The Moon's orbit is an ellipse so there are two focal points. One is the Earth, the place where we have incarnated. The other is Black Moon Lilith. She is a void, an Earth that is not there, the place of all that is missing...

43
The lunation cycle as a clown story

The Sun and the Moon are in a relationship.

Our parents embodied, to a certain extent, the energies of Sun and Moon.

They were more than just two distinct individuals. Mum and Dad were in a relationship.

Even if one disappeared never to reappear again, we knew we came from two.

Two sources exist within our souls.

Now, our parents were only representatives of the energies of Sun and Moon. We are children of Sun and Moon. We are children of Heaven and Earth.

The relationship between Sun and Moon in the horoscope is visible in the phases of the Moon: The New Moon occurs when Sun and Moon are conjunct, the Full Moon when they are opposed, the first and last quarter when they form a square.

The phase of the Moon we were born under is as meaningful as the signs and houses Sun and Moon are in. We are naturally attuned to what happens at this phase of the cycle.

If the Moon was alone, she would repeat the same patterns over and over again. If the Sun was alone, nothing would take shape.

When I was ten years old, I remember wondering:

> "Why do I have to go to school? I don't like sitting in a classroom all day long, that's not the life of my dreams! My parents are sacrificing themselves to enable me to go to school (that was the narrative...) They are sacrificing themselves so that I can have a

> *good job, earn money, get married, have children... and sacrifice myself in turn?!! What's the point? There must be more to life than repeating the same cycle again and again!"*

This was the Sun in me rebelling against the Moon. In principle, being a child, going to school, getting married and so on, could and should be a happy story. However, happy or not, the Moon only keeps the patterns of the past and reproduces them. As the saying goes: history repeats itself.

Is this all the Moon does? If she was alone, yes, that would be it. She has memory and reproductive powers.

The Sun, however, wants creation. Sun energy wants every one of us to shine in our own special way. The Sun wants individuality, or individuation.

The Sun can be understood as spirit.

Let there be light!

Let there be something new!

The Sun fecundates the Moon and the Moon will carry more than memories. She will receive the intention and power of the Sun as a seed and build forms for the purpose of manifestation.

Reading Rudhyar, I was craving for more illustrations. I came up with this one:

Clown lunation story

New Moon

One day a child was asked the question:
 "*What do you want to be when you grow up?*"
 The child said:
 "*I want to be a clown!*"
 "*A clown? Are you sure?*"
 "*Yes, I'm sure, that's what I want to be!*"

The Sun wants to become a clown. The Moon receives this seed-intention. She is the feminine principle. She gets fecundated. Let's make things happen now!

First Crescent:

Hey kid! You're really funny when you make faces in front of the mirror! Why don't you put on a little show this Sunday? Granny and Grandpa are coming for lunch, they would love to see a clown and have a good laugh."

"Oh, Mum I'm scared! Are my cousins coming as well? They are going to laugh at me! I don't want to!"

"Well, sweetheart, if you want to be a clown, you'll have to face the public one day! It's not too early to start!"

"Yes, but I'm scared!"

"It's going to be ok."

The New Moon was invisible. The first crescent is very thin, but the moon can be seen now. The little seed confronts reality for the first time. The dream of being a clown meets the old patterns.

"Is it bad to show off? Is my dream "ridiculous"? What ghosts of the past lie in wait for new dreams?"

First quarter

The child has been going to clowning workshops, has featured in local events, his budding talent has been acknowledged (and had all the school parents doubled up with laughter around the time the Sun and Moon formed a sextile). But now there is a serious decision to take. Taking it to the next level means going to a boarding school, far away from home. It's a special school where ten hours per week are dedicated to circus training. Fantastic atmosphere, great results. To become a clown, there is no better option. But Mum, teddy bear, Dad and friends have to be left behind. There will still be some weekends...

The first quarter is a time of crisis in action. It happens when the Moon and the Sun form the first square. In the sky, the Moon is exactly half illuminated, with a straight line dividing its luminous and obscure sides. This square is *"separating"*: The Moon is heading away from the Sun.

Gibbous Moon

Circus school headmaster talking:

"Hey, students! You've made a lot of progress. You have mastered all the basic skills you need to become circus artists. Now is the time to plan your first real show. Your audience won't be a supportive bunch of family members, but a real crowd of people who bought full price tickets and expect to get their money's worth. Let's get to work!"

This phase is a time of wilful activity oriented towards a goal that is now in sight. Dane Rudhyar compares the time of the beginning of this phase, which corresponds to a 135-degree angle (sesquisquare) to the time of the first crescent at a 45-degree angle (semi-square): with the first crescent, it was somehow the external world that opposed the growth of the new little thing; now, the new thing is much stronger and wilfully tackles the difficulties itself.

I am presenting these phases as a story in which things are going well. As you know, in life, that's not always the case. I could tell the story of a lunation cycle of doom and gloom another day. You can imagine. I'm just mentioning it here because all the artists are now suffering in the throes of stage fright. The curtain is about to rise.

Full Moon

The dream has come true. The clown is clowning. People are laughing. The new clown's inner child is exhilarated. Strangely, it's like the dream on one hand while on the other, not at all. Life is wonderful. You receive so much when you give! So much, so much...

Before the full moon, the energy was all focused on taking action. Building, making things happen. Personal development. Now, the time has come to offer the fruit. The time dedicated to self-development culminates as a relationship: a clown plays for an audience. Power is released.

The clown is thinking:

"This is only the beginning! What an experience!"

But the Moon is on the wane already.

The Full Moon is a new beginning. A new little seed has been sown, not a seed of more action to undertake, but a seed of consciousness.

What's the meaning of all this? What wisdom, what understanding of life will come from this? What will remain, in the soul, when it's all over? It's a little bit early to ask this question, but that's what is growing now: an understanding of the spirit of it.

Maybe the whole adventure of life is nothing but the story of spirit incarnating for the purpose of understanding itself.

The seed of consciousness will culminate at the next New Moon as the seed of the next cycle.

These questions will appear phase after phase. Now, the clown is just living life to the full.

Disseminating Moon

The Full Moon was really a peak, a moment of illumination! The public had never ever seen anything like that before!

Now the clown is known and loved by a wide audience. He gives interviews. He explains:

"There is much more to clowning than just being funny. A deep understanding of human nature is required. Clowning is a way to help people bear or even heal their sufferings, a way to pass essential messages, to get people to see things they wouldn't have wanted to look at without the help of a good laugh."

He is really on top of his game now. He can explain. He teaches classes, he inspires and he keeps disseminating all he can give.

The disseminating phase is to the Full Moon what the first crescent phase was to the New Moon. The new seed of consciousness, sown at the Full Moon, was entirely subjective; now, it meets the world for the first time and needs to demonstrate itself.

The clown keeps clowning. The years go by. New talents are appearing, and he is getting a little bit older.

Last quarter

"Already?"

Time passed so quickly... The children of today still like him. Kids like a clown that made their parents laugh. The world is changing. It's time to get used to the idea of retiring. How will the clowns of tomorrow look? Red noses and enormous shoes are so old school! Where will life be going tomorrow? Maybe there is a need for a complete reformulation of what clowning is all about... What being an artist is all about... What human life is all about...

The key word used by Dane Rudhyar in relation to the last quarter is *"crisis in consciousness"*. Leyla Rael uses the word *"re-orientation"*. What has been given has been. From the point of view of a growing consciousness, it's time to take some distance – the full commitment to action of the First Quarter becomes a full commitment to look at the bigger picture. Does it all make sense?

Balsamic phase

The clown is writing his memoirs. He thought of a title along the lines of: *"Message of an old clown to the world of tomorrow"*. He thinks of himself as a kind of Moses who walked all the way through the desert with his people and is about to die as the Promised Land is in sight. All his experiences,

The lunation cycle as a clown story

successes and failures, joys and pains, reflections and meditations boil down to (that's really the right word: *"boil down to"*) a few essential principles. Hopefully, his legacy will contribute to the joys, laughter and spiritual health of future generations.

Goodbye!

***

When we were born, the Moon and the Sun were at a particular phase of this Sun-Moon relationship story. For us, this phase is as important as our Sun sign, Moon sign and Ascendant.

Our Sun sign means that we were born during a particular season of the year, and more specifically when in that season: beginning, middle or end.

The zodiac and the seasons tell the whole story of life. Born under a particular sign we become *"the man of the moment"* or *"the woman of the moment"*. When life presents situations requiring someone just like us, we will fulfil the role!

The phase of the Moon we were born under has to be understood in the same spirit. Born under a waxing Moon, we are more action-driven; waning Moon people are more focused on understanding. If you understand the story of the whole cycle, you can easily figure out the personality traits which are characteristic of each phase.

To find out more, you may like to read *The Lunation Cycle* by Dane Rudhyar. I needed to imagine this clown story to understand better. However, if illustrations help clarify our understanding, they also come with a particular twist. Universal validity can only be expressed in the abstract. The lunation cycle applies to anything alive on this earth.

Moving to and fro from the most universal to the most particular and back, repeat...

Thank you for musing with me.

Every chapter of this book was first written as a blog post. However, to dive deeply into this world of symbols it's better to take our eyes off the screen.

Having a book in one hand and a cup of coffee, tea, or a healthy tisane in the other is a posture that is conducive to an enhanced state of consciousness!

May all the beings be happy, including you and me!

Jean-Marc

PS: You can find me online at: http://jeanmarcpierson.com

Ingram Content Group UK Ltd.
Milton Keynes UK
UKHW020357100523
421505UK00007B/107